T0159127

WISELY STUPID

Insight Is Wisdom
& Lack of It Is Not

BREEZE QUEEN

authorHOUSE®

AuthorHouse™
1663 Liberty Drive
Bloomington, IN 47403
www.authorhouse.com
Phone: 1 (800) 839-8640

Published by AuthorHouse 08/16/2018

ISBN: 978-1-5462-5611-3 (sc)
ISBN: 978-1-5462-5610-6 (e)

Print information available on the last page.

I dedicate this book to my husband, whose company I had always longed and would continue longing for the rest of my life, In spite of his abusive charm and incompletely fulfilled commitments he has brought to my life, a life worth living.

Author

Blessedness is not possession of material things, but blessedness is being contended with what one has.

Wrong thoughts can cause confusion leading to adverse circumstances.

Fear, doubt and indecisiveness can make a man weak and irresolute, which in turn can bring circumstances of failure.

Hatred and suspiciousness can cause accusations for others and self pitying for oneself, which can injure one's self confidence.

Righteous thoughts can bring grace and kindness, in turn invoking similar responses from others leading to congenial interpersonal relationships warranted for progress and harmony.

Mind controls the body and if a man is encompassed with fear, anxiety and doubts, they would demoralize him to make him react differently to unfavorable situations.

Relaxed mind reflects peace and healthy thoughts can bring cheerfulness and energy leading to happiness.

Fears and doubts have to be faced bravely otherwise they would allow avoidance behavior, making the subsequent tasks even more difficult and grave and there remains the possibility of continuously avoiding the same.

Oppression or submission to worldly authorities has to be discouraged and one can understand this strategy that both oppressors and sub missives are actually cooperating with each other in ignorance.

Uncongenial circumstances even present are not going to remain for long, as uncongenial environment provides time to develop latent powers and resources within ourselves.

The path of measures, struggles and sacrifices to live a life of calmness, adaptation, spiritual strength to increase a man's influence in society for permanent happiness, is the need of the time for believers.

In the name of God, the beneficent and merciful

I acknowledge my sincere thanks first to God, to have created and provided favorable circumstances to get this book published. I have to thank my husband for formality sake and I need to thank my children including in-laws for whom my migration took place and who are presently taking care of us.

Author

PREFACE

This is a story of my life having been transformed from an innocent girl to a woman of wisdom who is relying on gossip-oriented reports hinting towards insufficiently understood entanglements of marital companionships, warranting few dips into sins of indolence. In spite of the fact that the process of learning is difficult but their brilliant re-enactments of dramatized humility, which actually is a hope in search of contentment, which I got from the characters of this book.

Author

HUMILITY IN CELEBRATION

Words always need admiration of the virtues they possess and the courage they contain in them. The stories within stories it comprises of and little by little the incognito significance will get dawned on all. It will get transformed in all to act vigilantly and it will fight an un-ending war of their own causes and rights. Here is my story untold but known to all except those who are ignorant and who escape the liabilities they have to bear and live with. Everyone will receive extra-ordinary benefits from it, publicly or privately. I wanted to see if my valued writings and over valued conversations within myself will bring merits or demerits. Anywhere I go, they will feel fortunate rather than making me feel fortunate. My work is going to be immortal for all and it will a library of congress in itself, all pages filled and no page left unfilled.

My father was a thorough gentleman a gentleman who could be certified as a gentleman at any point of time day or night and he was a person with far sight and a person with a near sight. He was a pious man, a concerned father. A devout believer. A perfectionist, saint, an angel and a lesser god, as he presented himself to be.

He would cheat as much as he was allowed, he would fraud as much is feasible. He could bribe as much as he could afford. He was a semi-liar, complete boredom in a noun form. A semi-selfish man, a man who believed in gratification of his selfishly motivated aims and objectives.

He always undermined his wife. He considered her just some women, for service and even started calling his wife a 'woman'. A woman who in his books is meant for satiety of biological needs, a woman who is meant for sale of her service, a woman like a woman who was my mother, who was realistically, honestly and actually speaking, religiously was a thorough gentle lady, a God-fearing person. A person in veil like a curtain and a thick doubly woven cloth.

I belonged to a not so religious family. But a set of confessional traditional minds who may not know even the differentiation between religion and tradition. My father was a Veterinary assistant to hold cows, or sheep or chicken or some creatures godforsaken and untidily filthy miserable and poor. He managed to grab a piece of land left unoccupied by the fright of the people of my faith who fled to Partitioned country in a hurry leaving their lands vacant and my father sat on it and claimed to own it later by some state of artsy created, fake papers and constructed some hut like crumpled houses which were best suited to a water color painting by an immature artist who seemed as though was in a haste to complete it in time and sell it to be able to go to the nearest broth house.

My father was a bald, dark, graciously rouged looking person, who later constructed, rather improvised those mud houses, applied limestone powder and erected some catafalque like doors and planted a wild tree in the walkway and embarked upon a designation never suited to his image. Worst still he installed it beside the small gate. It reads 'Doctor so and so'. Who cares and who cared. We started living indoors and my brothers outdoor and my mother putting her feet into the log fire for cooking in a den. In a den like kitchen

My father raised some number of children out of his free time and donated some to some unconceived primitives. But an irony of facts was he loved them. I was supposed to assist my mother along with a retarded sister in household chores. House hold chores of cleaning the open space paved with rough unfinished factory rejected stones purchased from the nearest outlet in clearance sale open to sky with ugly twisted leaves falling from the tree so constantly for us to clean that I even thought of putting a net under the tree as shade to gather the fallen leaves for making my sweeping easier and to give the old broom stick some rest.

The chores also included collecting drinking water from hand pump placed in one of the corner of the space and to cut and chisel vegetables for the not so delicate or eatable, but my mother had to cook. The vegetables brought by the end of the month and meat brought by the beginning of the month mostly rotten, expired products warranting addition of extra spices to decorate the eatables and to hide the hideous taste to be able to swallow with gulps of water.

I was also supposed to assist my mother, off course without my retarded sister to wash clothes in another corner of the open space with a wooden handle not unlike the baseball bat to the hard stains of the clothes and to remove them by the mercy of harsh boric acid, bar soaps of some unknown company with very little water to rinse to be collected from the big water barrels. The collection itself, a challenging task leaving us with our skins to get darker and darker. We had a room or an ante-room or space converted into a room like provision with wooden bamboo sticking crossing each other at the back of the open space without doors or windows. The only windows we had were barred with iron rods at the front of the house to look out into the lane but we were not supposed to peep as our brothers living outdoors if see us would beat the shit out of us.

We people met in circumstances, where performances were mixed with evaluations of challenges. Evaluations were subdued by distractions and were not carried forward. There can be seriousness to the deal, things were dealt seriously and concealed by silent happenings, trivial enough to occupy time and time alone. Passing time on the other hand has taught me the adaptive learning of confusion. Confusions about differences of values, our values labeled as issues or non-issues. No doubt differences existed, but I did not value the initiation of the same. I also did not value the truth to make a family, that marriage was a product of my choice.

Talking about nature's calls, we had a short-time squatting hole to use behind a swinging metallic rusted door only half covered as you see open from up and down. Like you see in western cowboy films when rouges enter and escape from. It was funny how, when in use we could know by the feet seen from the outside as to who has occupied. We also had a tiny bathroom attached to toilet where water was filled in similar metallic drums with a centrally placed platform of cement to sit and bathe ourselves and water to be rinsed, through small mugs against which I would have preferred diving and dipping and struggling to come out to dry ourselves with papery thin cotton towels with impressions of wild animals and while rubbing our back I sometime notice the wild animal's claws abrading my back and off course the upper opening of the door helping us to hang our clothes old and new, soiled or fresh to be replaced before being worn. What a glamorous life I had had in my childhood.

I was lean, thin and under-nourished, but must have been pretty looking in my own way to attract boys and men crossing the street, some vendors who were called to stop at our door to sell amenities collected from some second-hand market. We used to like selecting small items of our interest from combs to plastic dolls and candies. Once one vendor gave me a large sugar candy and assured me to enjoy, while he himself was trying to collect coins from my shirt pockets, which we had many. He was taking time searching for the money and I was cherishing the taste of sugar candy dissolving in my mouth. This was a life we lived in childhood, leveled to like it with the limited blessings we were showered on.

We later moved to our grand father's house, next lane, which was already inhabited by several families all living together like herds of animals. There was scarcity of space in rooms and small open yard covered by a thick hand-woven curtain from tween thread curtain to maintain privacy from on lookers of the street. The rooms were small, dark and over-stuffed with belongings. We started living with uncles, aunts, and many cousin brothers and sisters. Some un-invited guests also used to spend nights while moving towards their own shelters in the nearby villages or districts. Our grandfather's den where we were housed was a mess in literal sense.

That was the time when ink pens were common man's utility item and ball point pens were a luxury for the affluent. Only later the history was reversed more than history getting repeated and ball point pens became a common utility and ink pens became a luxury for their usage. Usage in its correct composition than use. I don't like these times. I also don't know how to present as I learned English only after migration and needed translation of my thoughts and idioms.

The joint family hosing remained a chaos, while we would be crumpled all together to sleep or half-asleep or half-awake with hypnogogic hallucinations and we were kicked, man-handled, massaged and palpated by unseen and unknown hands. Those were unpleasant touches, terrible fun and horrific joy. I couldn't understand then but understood now. Life goes on and I went with it. I attended school interruptedly, only walking distance from home, carrying my back-pack of books, behind the scarf and used to return when my hoodlum brothers were not around. My mother used to give me some snacks kind of things again under the scarf and we lived on.

I grew up tall and elegant enough to start getting proposals for marriage from neighbors, distant relatives and even some strangers. My father was in urgency to send me away. Those were the trends too. My father would have given me in marriage against the first proposal received, if not for my underage and he could have gone to the municipal records to amend my age if required by the needs of the time. I couldn't blame him for he had another liability of my retarded sister to be sent away. Those were the times when postponement of decisions used to become liabilities. Girls were sitting at home for want of dowry payments and better posted candidates would ask for handsome dowries even if they themselves were not handsome. It was the trend of the society we lived in.

One of my cousin brother, first or second, I don't know, got hold of a government job by way of corruption, which was a routine in those times. The greater amount you pay the better job you may have. He was proposed for me and my father was thinking in his favor not for anything, except his government posting. We grew up together and also played together, but I never had any interest in him, neither he showed any, until of late he got attracted as all others and feared that he would miss me if he delays his proposal. He was under consideration and remained for quite some time. With passing time, I was growing up and his interest too. But nothing materialized.

It was a matter of chance or luck that one proposal came from nowhere about a Doctor working abroad and my father decided to accept it even without exploring the family background. The name of his father was enough of a consolation. The biodata was impressive notifying his father who had been a police officer and a celebrity of his times, awarded gold medals. His grandfather was from Bombay also awarded with a street to his name. I was shown a passport size photo of the Doctor, who looked good if not handsome but I wondered why he was wearing sunglasses. Maybe due to the photo having been taken in the bright lights of the studio or he was gifted one recently which he wanted to try on and see how it reflects.

In any case I wanted to look into eyes. I was told eyes speaks for themselves. Eyes reflect the basic personality. Eyes are wisdom or stupidity. As I had a fear of Doctors, for either they give bitter suspensions or painful injections. Even if there is an abrasion or a small laceration, instead of being tender they rub vigorously, pretending to clean the wound and would put a suture or two if required or not. They have their own apprehensions and they infect their fears into others. I don't know why people say, half of their illness goes away upon seeing a Doctor. May be, it has some placebo effect or may be, they get an ear to listen to their pains and sufferings. I didn't want to marry a person whom I fear.

Fates were destined. My father fixed the date of the marriage, as a prior understanding and even to print the invitation cards as a pre-requisite to be sent to the Doctor to show to the authorities and get some kind of emergency leave to come for marriage. Telegrams were exchanged and we all awaited his arrival. He was working somewhere in north Africa and it was far off. I think he was also sent my passport size photo which he approved and he was coming for the ceremony. I didn't know anything about marital intimacies or intricacies. Sex education was not taught in schools those days. Elders were inhibited to discuss such issues among themselves, leave alone the children.

I was getting married to a stranger, with zero knowledge of what would take place thereafter. I was also getting afraid of leaving the familiar surroundings and especially my mother, who always used to protect me. There are limits of everything but she used to embrace me our of my fear of thunder storms, which lasted with me, as I was not exposed to it. I had not even traveled in city bus to old city's lord bazar, a lady's favorite place to purchase anything which a woman would like to have or would love to see, window shopping. I was told I will have to fly back to reach my would-be, I mean Doctor.

One fine morning my parents were riding on their moped motor cycle, which no doubt runs on petrol, but also could be peddled to any destination, if petrol gets exhausted. They were to meet the Doctor, who visited last night from his place of work. In no time they returned obviously happy to have met him and okayed an already okayed match. I heard they were discussing their good luck to have gotten such a good proposal. I wonder how people could jump to conclusion so fast. Next moment there was a flood of relatives and the mood was jubilant. There was a short time left to complete thousand and one arrangements for pre-wedding and post-wedding celebrations.

I recollected my mother's words which needed appreciation, as she could see through from her veil at the Doctor, during the briefest interaction she had and narrated his type as a reserved type. I liked reserved people as they would be listeners, would have a poise in them and presence too. I was not sure of the under-current happenings but I was beginning to like him. He was not wearing his goggles then and my parents could see clearly that there was no lazy eye or squint and he appeared to be plain and simple type, who attended the meeting with a pant, a T shirt and a pair of slippers. He did not try hiding his effected limb that one, which was little shorter than the other. But who cares or who would have noticed if he would have been wearing shoes on. Things were made easier for every one to analyze before concluding.

GROUNDED REALITIES

2

I want to register some facts of my life. I want to share my conviction of dignity and fame which my writing will acquire in the end. It will be a renaissance and a revolution of this century. Words are used for their literary meaning and not as metaphors. All used to be seduced by the way I walk, talk and stand and bend. It will be the fidelity of sovereign faith and freedom, not very outside their confines. It will get confirmed in the end, with all to avail a free will and not to dissolute its worth. The prospects which are being taken will consume several centuries of wisdom at its peak. I had to spell out my thoughts, my reasoning, my striptease of secrets, fact by fact and truth by truth.

I collected this information in bits and pieces. I was made aware of these facts that Doctor also had a humble beginning. He was very young when he was afflicted by post- polio paresis and his father was killed in an unfortunate tragic accident. His father had two wives and Doctor's biological mother was the younger one. Both the young wives were widowed at a very young age and were left to raise two orphans on their own. Because of his father's short service span and time of death away from duty, during leisure hours, created a very limited pension amount for the family's survival. That was I believe post partition time and people were fleeing to the neighboring country and there was no one left for them to help.

Times lapse, realizations were seen and procedures enacted. I never wanted to judge that this relationship should be disclosed as choices of people involved and I never wanted to be taken for granted. The fact of the matter is, it was never taken for granted; it could not have been taken as it is, until approved by me. Parents see some chemistry of reception on two sides. Humbly I requested for something and subtly they wanted it some other way. I respected their wishes and the subdued reasons of the same even centered my ideologies. We went along, other interested parties kept coming and we kept refusing on the assumed exchange of formalities and kept happily declining the fixations till my marriage was fixed with Doctor.

Some American missionary took care of his orthopedic surgeries and he was able to walk with a slight swaying of his left limb but had to walk long distance to school. There was very little that he could do but continued his struggle, under the umbrella of scholarships, book funds, charitable organizations and mercy of God. It proved a drastic downfall from normalcy for him and he became very sensitive. There were times when he would not get lunch and he used to assist affluent students in doing their assignments for some returns, but meagre returns. He started giving private tuitions to students of primary and secondary schools at home getting some remuneration, which he used to pass on to his mother for home needs.

Both the widows started living, sharing each-others sorrows and hardships and developed a strong bond among themselves. He started painting in leisure time and used to make water color sketches of stills and landscapes to sell at his friend's book store for extra money. He had a talent for singing and was awarded several prizes in vocal music competitions but he could not pursue his talent for want of money to purchase a second-hand harmonica. He had a big circle of friends and was popular among them. His ability to maintain wit and humor was entertaining his friends circle always. After hearing his initials days of hardship, I was already developing a soft corner for him. Not that

I suffered as he did, but I had a liking for people who don't lose hope and continue their efforts in life without worrying for the results.

I was told he used to study hard and got admission into medical school through merit, but he used to go to his college by cycle, iron his white medical student's coat by keeping folded under his pillow to get the creases out. He never bothered for clothes, as he couldn't afford them. I believe he was not happy that his mothers sacrificed their lives for him. He would have preferred them to find better matches and settle their own lives. He was always concerned towards them and worry a lot to keep them happy. His mothers were abandoned by their relatives, who migrated to the divided part of the sub-continent and got occupied in their own problems. People do not consider their obligations.

I was told he was working since morning giving tuitions to young kids, then would go to his medical school in the mornings, afternoons were occupied by clinical postings in the hospital and evenings were obligatory for him to work as correspondent in some staff college and in the nights, he was working as billing clerk in his friend's hotel. Must be hard for him to run this routine every day for so long. After he was qualified as a Doctor he did his internship and by that time he managed to purchase a second-hand scooter to go long distances, for which he felt relieved. He completed his course got certification for his qualifications and had three offers of jobs from abroad. He rejected the job of kingdom of Saudi for its harsh weather, wanted to go to Trinidad but could not afford the ticket and left with no other option except to take up this present posting in north African province of Libya.

He learnt Arabic spoken language and was easily mistaken for a local Libyan. He was posted initially in emergency hospital and he was working there living with his bachelor friends from home town. That was the time I was getting married to him and to his good luck he got transferred to his faculty of choice, Psychiatry and was transferred to the local psychiatric facility in suburbs. He purchased a beetle foxy Volkswagen car and used to drive alone working from 8 am to 2 pm. He was given accommodation in pre-fabricated housing colony nearer to airport and his flat was on the third floor. He used to carry groceries and even gas cylinder on his own without depending on anybody. I believe he was liked by all, authorities and sub-ordinates.

I was happy for he expected change and was enjoying comments from my peer group that I am going to be a Doctor's wife. My aunts and cousin sisters took me to the bathroom and applied turmeric and sandal wood powder, scrubbed my body and bathed me vigorously, against my wish. I felt no big need for all these rituals, but it was a relaxing and soothing experience. We all got busy in pre- arrangements and pre-wedding ceremonies. There were women folk singing folk songs and some girls were even trying to dance to the rhythm of the beats. My father had already booked the local community hall for the occasion and similarly the groom's side had booked another community center nearby. The religious ceremony was peaceful and I was supposed to be lifted by the groom and to be carried to the car to be carried to the in-law's house.

Doctor was reluctant to hold me in public and must have been worried to hurt me if he trips with me and we both fall. My cousin brother who was actively participating in the wedding activities offered his service and Doctor was relieved to hand over the responsibility of lifting the bride, by his gesture of hand of welcome, a tradition which could have been avoided altogether. But curiously it fulfilled his intention to make me his bride and for a transient time he was actually performing the ritual, except while keeping me seated in the car he knocked my head to the car door and I felt giddy. We went to Doctor's apartment in a posh colony where he had recently purchased it after working abroad. It was located at the second floor and had balconies on both sides. Another adjacent empty apartment was taken in their custody for our placement of privacy and rooming capacity needs.

He was a strange man in the crowd, who got immersed in my heart from my eyes. Seeing him with graceful glances my own verses became still in my lips. I imagined some poetic verses which did not match his elegance and his sophistication. They became the height of any praise worthy of poetry and he had a unique style of narration which crossed he boundaries of excellence and reward. Each word seemed to be a moon light to me and his every speech was the height of wisdom for my standard. He was like sparkling reflection of my own dreams which beautified my own reflection of his imagination for me. Whatever I could write in his worth or whatever I could speak for his priceless self, had actually cherished my fondness and my delight was brightened. I found myself a blessed soul.

Both me and Doctor were exhausted and we slept well after praying together. The next day was also made hectic by people from his side visiting to see the bride and to bless the couple. I was fed some food by Doctor's cousin sisters and in the evening was the pre-arranged reception dinner party. I was already tired and vexed by the continuity of traditional ceremonies, exhausted by the heat of heavy clothing, the repetitive exposure of my face to the visiting women folk and right at the dinner time, I fainted. Before Doctor could have been called, my elder mother-in-law gave me a decoction and I felt better. It was unusual of brides to faint, but I must have been dehydrated or just tired in excess or the untoward effect of mild head injury sustained a day before, when I was being put to car by my cousin brother. Things moved smoothly then and we returned home.

Doctor was scheduled to go back to work abroad after two days and we were happy to exchange love, care, concern, very little but gainful talks and he took out mouth freshener and sprayed into his mouth. I was mistakenly afraid that he may do the same to me and then may advantage of my unconsciousness. I have heard stories of rape conducted after making girls unconscious. But nothing of that sort took place and next day I didn't remain a virgin anymore. I was aghast and confused about what was taking place, but time passed by quickly and we slept again for longer time, until knocked and awakened. How quickly another day passed and he was packing to go back to Libya. I don't know why, but I cried and cried. My mother was called to console me but she could not help it.

The time of his departure approached and we all went to the adjacent airport to send him off.

There were no emotional scenes or melodramas which took place. Everybody was busy doing their gestures of farewell. Doctor looked at me and I noticed a world of understanding in his eyes. He waived all of us and crossed the gate. We returned home and I started living in that well-lit, airy and cozy atmosphere. I remembered Doctor's advice to start writing a journal or diary in my spare time, about whatever happens in his absence, to while away time and to let it work as catharsis for any worries I was lodging in new surroundings. I had just one problem and that was being unaccustomed to sleep alone. I started sleeping with my younger mother-in-law and it was a relief. I had good time, except getting lonely, but there was an adjacent market to go and balconies to view the outside activity.

My mother-in-law took me to the nearby bank and opened an account in my name and started depositing monthly allowance as my pocket money. We were visiting places, my family started visiting me and time was passing at a slow pace. My elder mother-in-law had a pet cat and she used to talk to her, as though conversing with a friend. I was getting acclimatized with the new surroundings and new routine. There was a phone at home but no provision of long distance calling facility. I had to wait for letters to arrive to know the sequence of events. I was feeling little awkward about getting married and left alone. But I was told that he had to submit the paperwork to arrange for my visa to join me. I used to eagerly wait for the postman to come and postman was equally eager to collect tips on bringing letters from abroad.

One fine morning the postman was at our door with a big envelop and a big smile. He new he will get a tip today. I was thrilled but found out that the airport visa papers were for Doctor's elder brother who wished to go to Libya and help his family to survive. Doctor had an obligation for the same and had notified to me in an earlier letter. I had forgotten getting carried away by wishful thinking. But the sequence of events which followed were his elder brother went and in no time came back, either he was not qualified for the job or didn't like the place. Doctor had sent my airport visa papers through him and I was to go ultimately.

As such it had taken a long time and my waiting was stretched for too long. I was almost getting bored of waiting, bored of the routine, bored of filling my diary pages and bored of the news of the world. TV channels aired the news that people can stay fit without suppressing appetite, and I found it so ambiguous that I thought news media was not able to suppress their appetite for such news. There was another item that poor dental health can frail ageing person's body and mind, as if good dental health can increase the quality of ageing and decorate the quantity of ageing. There was a slogan which was being watched like having become viral that peace can heal stress and tranquility can peel peace, but these newsies were only able to evoke worries and nothing else.

Some anchor was telling that 8 hours of sleep is compulsory and important for living, as though if someone has to struggle in excess to live normally, it is not possible, but what Doctor has told me that number of hours of sleep are not relevant to the well being of body and mind. I couldn't understand the news about clean children and unclean leaders are getting involved in scams. So, in other words clean people are reasoning out with unclean methods to clean the images of unclean censors of clean services to unclean shadows. Someone was saying records are meant to be broken and broken records are meant to be fixed and expatriates are earning millions by migration to prosperous countries from under-developed countries.

Judicial storms started taking place after economic storms, poverty storms, snow storms, thunder storms, etc., by communal elements of original separatists and changing the unanimous unions vouched for the undocumented. I failed to understand what they mean and what they intend to convey. Presidents are labelled capitalists and prime ministers are being called communists, actually described as capitalists being mis-spelled by their own people as communists and military dictators are unwilling to leave their posts in spite of protests and are abusing people with no intention of learning and the locals of attacked countries are being given asylum in developed countries and are being supported by the commons of the world. Well I didn't care. I was to reach Doctor. Tickets were booked and the news spread and a rush of visitors started to come.

I was travelling for the first time by air, or for that matter travelling alone. I didn't know anything about aero planes except that I used to see them landing and taking off from the back side of our balcony, rather expecting for the Doctor's plane to land someday, instead I was supposed to take off to go to him, somewhere in Libya. Suitcases were packed, families gathered, and I was carried to airport. One of our neighbors was an officer at the airport and he was of big help in seeing me off. Photos were taken of garlanding and I was the last to climb the stairs and after saying each other that God will remain our guardian, I was air borne and my plane took off. I did not forget to pack my dairy and to look through the pages filled.

HEARTFELT AFFECTATIONS

Dear Doctor,

What did you do to me. You appeared from no where and vanished in thin air. You went several seas apart, but how come you magnetized me like a magnet and I was getting attracted towards you inch by inch. You magnified me like a fascination. You did some magic on me that I developed so intense feelings for you. Now I cannot see anything except you. Your handsomeness and your grace full features. Living around my own people I felt lonely and living amongst acquainted surroundings I was strangely isolated. Almost secluded in my thoughts about you. How tenderly you cared for me, how delicately you balanced your concern for me sharing a major portion with me.

You passed some poetic verses in my appraisal which mystified me to the extent that I only imagined the enjoyment I had in your company. I realized you were an inspirational source of adoration for me, which continued to reverberate within me a liking towards life. Love for birds, love for breezes, love for flowers and you. You were to love and also to be loved. For the first time I understood the meaning of attachment, the depth of concept of belongingness. I know you can hide your feelings and you did not show it and did not express it. Your looks with your arms around your chest were like open arms to embrace me. We did not spend a long time together, but it was enough to captivate me forever.

This togetherness I dream can be stretched for long and very long time and I am still dreaming with my open arms for you and for the warmth of your care. I imagine you holding me lightly tight, brushing aside the swirls of curling hair, which were falling upon your tantalizing appeal for me and I am still feeling captivated by the same, which calls upon to let me fly along with the flows of tides to reach you. You went so far that I wanted to free myself like the feathers of the bird, desperately trying to fly to come closer to you. But in spite of having gone so far, I feel close to you and your fragrance. Your gazes, gestures and smiles inviting me to join you.

It looks now as if you have covered me with your coziness of affection, which I found for the first time in my life. I wait upon the postman to bring me your chits of syllables adding themselves to convey your lovely charm making me feel satisfied with satiety and fulfilment. My goal is to follow your footsteps to reach you and get noticed to be a part of commendable warmth you left in me. I remembered your sprinkling of your affection to your mothers, your family, friends and neighbors and sometimes even strangers included who casually visited you but returned with your gift of kindness and sympathy, they deserved. I wonder from where you brought all those gifts, gifts of values, virtues and consideration you always carried with you.

You cherished me to be in your company with generous comfort and convenience. Come back and carry me to distances, where no one can find us and we would stroll holding hands together day and night. Through the paths paved by green mountains, blue seas and colorful flowered gardens, me clinging to you and you allowing me to cling to you. Cling for no more separation. Carry me to the dreamland in which you are living all by yourself and your dreams are giving a cool shade in which I am dissolving myself. Your paths are my destinations your call my goal. Come back and carry me in your protective arms and let us fly to nowhere to get lost in time and space. I want to get absorbed in you and get amalgamated in your luster to become one part, never to get distanced again.

I wish you come back once and for all, come back for good, so that we hide under the roof of gray clouds and take peaceful rest underneath the shade of drizzles yet to fall and get wet, drenched with each other's adoration to walk in the coolness you possessed for me. I am obsessed with repetitive fancies about you and no body except you. I wish to hide behind your blessings sampled in these gestures which appear as though written in my blood-stained phrases, which is getting splattered on paper giving a pinkish background to ask upon you to come back. I am willing to put my heart out covered in an envelop to apply some irrevocable glue to send you, immaterial of my fear of losing it.

I am living in constant dread of my feeling about me getting lost in the distance created by this world between us. I may get lost to be carried by winds to you, hidden in this dazed sphere of subtle unclear space separating us. I want to get lost to lose myself within yourself. Let us travel together any distance anywhere, but don't leave me behind to cry in solitude waiting for you, thinking about you and planning togetherness again. I want this togetherness so fixed, so constant and so compact that no force can separate us. I may lose myself to get you back or you come back and take me. Take my thoughts in your possession, my feelings and my passion for you and keep me with you. Embrace me tightly forever.

Let us sing a song in the form of a duet merging rhymes and rhythms of melody into one long lasting song, irresistible to stop singing together, embracing and dreaming together. I dream that we are swinging in the rainbows slowly holding together and then taking long swings to leap across the moon and stars, brushing past the clouds to remain in that space investing each other's wants in each other and to rise above the horizons to get lost but holding each other. Carry me to remain in each other's company budding and emerging fondness to last forever. Let us lose our sorrows and grief of separation and let us not look back what we have left behind.

My arms are still stretched in my dreams wide apart groping for your encirclement. You are my newly found solace which I don't want to lose. You are a valuable lost for me, a treasure lost for me and heavenly desire lost for me. I aspire your calm warmth and your affection, in which you have immersed me and given me a shelter, which has become my life, my desire and my immense wish and I don't want it to be broken again. Squeeze me to get your scented flavor to preserve me in it and let me lie beside you inhaling the fragrance filling my senses for my utmost satisfaction.

Yours forever.

I filled the first few pages of my diary written in my local dialect of Urdu. I felt better. It was a good advice parted by Doctor. I decided to continue writing but would forget mostly the details of day to day activity. So, I was irregular with my assignments. After few days I wrote another letter.

My dear Doctor,

What would sane people know about self-involvement in personal thoughts and feelings of a person who is so quickly deprived of the righteous company of a partner. They would know only if they are placed in my situation, having undergone the exchanges we underwent, me and you. How would they know that after meeting your gazes and looks, the dim star was fully lit and how would they know what is the magical influence of being loved? I was astounded by the happening that I could not confide my feelings for you and you might have thought silence was the answer to my expressions unspoken. My open swirls of curly hair might have taught poetry to the seasons, but my half-closed eyes with slant stares should have made you understand what likeness is, what is affection and intimacy means to me.

As such you are far away as though standing at the shore not even seeing that I am downing but not drowned completely. I am sub-merging and surfacing to make belief that I could forget the time spent in togetherness. I knew it is not related to your cruelty but you were equally afflicted in the same way, I feel but you had obligations to fulfil. Keeping things to yourself, as a sequence to compromise with the prevailing times, you were compelled to leave me and not on intention and you did not feel defeated. Now if the world would like to label me insane let them do, people are cruel and they can make up stories. I may be insane but not a puppeteer showing a show. I should not bother for the people's interpretation. They are spectators for entertainment.

I shouldn't be predisposed by the separation anxiety I am suffering with in my relation to yours. Please do not ponder me with these feelings anymore for any reason. I wish time gets installed and clocks stop moving to give me some relief of my suffering, but my heart is still racing to join you, so that I could spell out my thoughts which I lodge within me for you. Help is not forgetting this anguish, which is tormenting me and would not do so if I try to dampen your memories. I don't even intend to call upon your attention to distract you from your responsibilities, but I can't help that I can't stop me from thinking about you. I didn't have any reason to show urgency in meeting with you, except that I was looking for excuses to justify this forced separation forced upon me and with which I have to live by, I don't know for how long.

Whenever I see our album of photos of wedding and the post wedding events, I get thoughts about you. I imagine me exposed to harsh sun and you trying to cover me as a cool shaded tree. Every day I desire to be with you and every night I convince me of the conditions unfavorable still to be faced. Only after you left I realized what I found and what I lost. I wonder why time is singing a rhyme which we couldn't participate into. I feel I have no friends and no enemies around and I admonish that this city has become estranged to me. There was a time we appreciated our longingness for each other up to a stage of insanity and now I am left with parting from you and I consider this as my destiny. I cannot ask anyone to relieve me as each one has their own distresses and sorrows to live with. I cannot confide in anyone as all are so distant with me, except you and even in spite of distance I feel closeness and could confide in you. That amount of trust you have infected in me.

At time I get inconsolable thoughts that you were made for me, created for me, before we met you were some where hidden in galaxy and then you were called to step down to the earth for me. Your person, body and mind are my property, your kindness and your considerate looks are my possession, your talks and your listening attitude was for me. I feel melodious music is echoing In the surroundings and I am curling up to look back at your grace. I have a feeling that you will keep me company for the rest of my life and you will continue to glance at me with plea and appeal for my love for you, which I have preserved in my heart for you forever.

I feel you should not have insisted to leave, instead you should have remained beside just beside me and I think I may die and I may be stolen if I cannot find you beside me. The times of our togetherness were spent so quickly and so quickly the separation became imminent. You think for yourself why I shouldn't restrain you, as the mere thought of distancing with you arise a fear in me. Life is time bound and we had only few moments of liberation to interact with each other and after losing those moments I am thirsty of your attention and care. How innocent and colorful was the time when you were around and it was the height of a combination of my beauty and your love and who know when we could meet again and I wanted to freeze those memories for you.

Yours loving wife

My diary was filling up scrap notes. I thought I would show him some day to make believe my thinking of the past memoirs. I got preoccupied in preparations to join him. The diary was left untouched. Many a times I opened to scribble down my thoughts but kept delaying it. I found chance again and I wrote.

My Doctor, my life,

I am not feeling well, rather I am feeling sad. Sad like crying. There were many excuses for me to cry, but what refrained me was to respect your prestige and position and the adoration for your love towards me. You yourself said to me that crying upon mishaps doesn't help and that note alone didn't let me cry aloud. I used to sob in seclusion. I would surely cry upon meeting you as I couldn't during your last short visit with time constraints. I feel like conveying to people who could afford to cry, to let them cry on my behalf, as I cannot bear anymore your separation and lack of your company.

I am sure you don't have any prejudices against anyone, more so towards me then come back to leave me again. My expectancy of heartfelt feelings would continue to expect from you to takeover all my worries and to light a candle of hope, which I can reconcile by letting you to come back to extinguish it.

Since long I deprived myself of the privilege of crying not to let my pent-up frustrations get subjected to catharsis, but now my soul and my life come back to gift me the honor of crying in your arms and crying upon your shoulder. You may consider the enormity of my liking for you, so consider me as angry upon your departure and keeping away from me and come back to console me and lean upon me to light my joy. I know you are a reserved person and it is your way of hiding affection, which is affection in itself, but some day casually come back and let me remind me of your hidden affection for me. I know you have justifications for not coming back, so soon, but come back and justify not returning back from me.

Thanks God I am still living and what else can I tell you. With the traditions of time, now I am able to understand the delicacies of relation keeping and moreover with passing time I am also forgetting the crave of my longingness for you. The atrocities of life or the adversaries of my conscious, what should I bear this or that. I would have cried and remembered you, if I could have been provided by the privacy of being with myself. Some customs should witness my feelings and record them as to how much penalties I am allocated with

Yours lovingly.

MINDFUL MISUNDERSTANDINGS

Doctor,

Do you have some spare time, if so, then listen to what I have to tell you? I am getting thoughts like are not letting me see living is difficult or easy without you, people are commenting that I am little tensed up. You have provided a path for me to follow upon you, but I want to see why it has become tortuous and empty. It looks like people are again being cruel to me, not just people but the circumstances also and I want to see whether this is intended for my destruction. Underneath these candles which are lit to spread light, why there is darkness underneath them, I want to see why and even you may wonder why.

I know you are not stranger to me anymore, but I still want to see, if there can be seen a closer connection which I am missing out. Your appraisals for me, your considerations, my requests and my appeals, I want to see how far they can convince me to find peace and tranquility of my fears and anxieties and impending depression. I want to see all by myself and want to be sure of the conditions whether they were inevitable or imposed upon me as tests and trials.

Sometimes I wonder why I am in search of you and your appearance, more so when the strings of the instrument are broken, why there are some musical notes still are being generated out of it. If someone ask me about my immediate future, what could I say and it was good of them that they have not asked me as why to my heart had developed a bleak crackle in it. I know you have not done this on purpose, you have not broken my heart for any reason, how can I explain and justify the broken pieces scattered all around me.

I am standing on a fork of a way of my life and I wonder why I am being carried away by the whimsical desires I want to get satisfied with. I am ashamed that at the same time while I am concerned about my desires you are occupied in earning our livelihood for future. I also wonder why I am not left with any wish or hope of reunion, as the time is passing by and the fact is, only patience is warranted out of our affairs to become fruitful.

It looks sometimes as if everything has died within me, but then why this soul-less body is still lying without a coffin.

It looks as if I am changing, my thinking is changing, Doctor, I am almost thinking as you used to think. I received your letter, but I could not add up my chit in the bulk of chits usually sent all together. I don't like the ways all others are following, I don't like to walk on paths which are tampered with, listening to wrong talks and nodding my head silently as before, no doubt they had their own advantages but I don't like it any more. I am beginning to expect self-respect in enemies and let it be no more bending and yielding to cruelty, which I am beginning to dislike. To me those people who bear and live with such things are like the tendrils which have risen from the ground flavored with the scent of fresh growth and later had become independent and started to dislike the roots from where they have risen up. I would tell the people who have lighted fire to burn a colony, that my own house which was left unharmed which, I don't like.

Whose sorrows I am perceiving and shedding tears for, what are these tears and to what agony they have witnessed, is it my tender-hearted view or love for humanity that these tears are a proof of my association with civilization in which I am living. These tears which I am shedding for others, are rising a feeling in my heart towards kindness for others, towards the suffering of others, that for other's sad stories these tears are bulging out of my eyes. Are these tears only just are secreted from my lacrimal glands that are hurt by other's gloom, then I feel like asking these tears that this story has just begun, does that mean that these tears were non-existent before.

I have my own doubts that these tears were hidden somewhere, between my eyes and my heart waiting to be shed. In between these distances are dreams of cities and fulcrum of thoughtfulness, where love is entangled between roses and thorns, and further to these roses are forests of turmoil, I think these tears were installed somewhere there and some traumatic event has let them flood into my eyes and some painful experiences have brought them to the brink of my eyelashes, I feel proud of these tears who were on their way stopping and progressing and stopping. Waiting for some sad story to bud up and to let these tears find their way to overflow from my eyes, I some time ask such questions myself in solitude.

Yours patient.

I think I was sad and depressed, but those mood swings are normal for my conditions and circumstances. I was afraid Doctor may misunderstand my feelings. I gave some gap in noting my feelings in the diary.

My Doctor,

It is quite some time that I did not receive any message from you, to which I wait every day. But I can understand you are all by yourself struggling for family's sake and I have become an additional liability on you. Do not try to hide your feelings with me. I have come to know your type. Thinking about you I am getting a perspective of what you are. As far as I am concerned, I can adjust to any change and any deviation. I am a voice and a different voice, which does not have to accommodate to migration. I am destined to be a migrating bird and most girls are. God has brought me to this stage, that my shadow also climbs over me to cross me.

I sometime feel something inside me had broken without any noise and outside me there a lot of noises taking place. I am not a coward to yield to any adversary, I prefer waiting to fight the real hardships of life, yet to be borne. Who doesn't like to smile, but life should provide a chance to smile. I imagine myself walking on stray paths and when I want to return I am not finding way back home. I can even change the ways of my following and I have the capacity to get away from these distressing thought, of this sustained separation with you. I have pen at my disposal and the characters which I can shape and if I want I may even change the story's ending as well.

I sometime feel I have a different retrospective of myself than the sun itself, where it sets it has to rise from the other side but I can set and rise from the same side. I got a question whether hope is essential or perseverance is essential for life and I found myself writing an answer to the same since long. I am like a barren land colored by my shades and I am trying to fill the sky with same colors. From the creases of my reflection in the mirror I seem to have appeared to see my own reflection very different than what it was. I seem to be writing the story of my life and where there was pain hidden I was writing it as remedy. I would keep your advice close to my heart but you may know that I can rebel if need arise. You may not have heard the sound of my heart breaking but I have the capability to get mixed with the chill laughter around me.

Yours forever.

I was getting curious thoughts and I felt like penning them down.

My life and soul,

I am curious to know and you may interpret these thoughts for my benefit. I know God is merciful. He has given provisions to his creations all that makes them feel good. But I feel I am getting poetic. I was getting inspired by J. Akhter's poetic verses. The jest of what I understood is the following.

There came an order that all breezes which are flowing across freely had to forecast their directions and also have to notify their speed. In spite of the fact that there is hurricane non-existent but the ruler is worried that the walls he has erected around his fortress and the dwellings he has made out of cardboards, which he found it a requirement to protect himself and his forces and he is well aware of his long-time animosity with winds which lose their control and destroy the fabrications.

There was a co-existent order that waves and flow of the rivers also should keep themselves within their limitations and their rise and fall of waves in beyond acceptance and indicative of rebellion and wrong doing, all seem like restlessness and viciousness and rebellion cannot be granted permission to bud up, and the order was to keep the rivers within their boundaries if at all they want to survive, they have to flow silently without making any noise.

There was yet another order that gardens can only blossom the flowers of a single shade and the rulers will decide the color for them and what sort of gardens are permissible to be grown and blossom their flowers. Beyond doubt the flowers will remain only single colored, but the shade they contain, how deep or shallow they would be. How could the rulers be notified that the flowers in any garden cannot remain within their contrasts of colors, they just cannot be. That colors are reflections of their bounty and independence, which cannot be captured and with in a color are hidden many shades of color.

Let the rulers know that those of them who gave such order if and executed and get flowers of single colored flower, how intense would be the scene and how desperate they became thereafter. How could somebody inform them that breezes, rivers and gardens do not listen to order other than that of nature and nature is governed by God's rules only. Breezes cannot be captured in jails to restrain their flow, and when waves stop flowing their currents, whatever may be the rivers width and depth, it gets ridiculed and undermined. And they should know that the first step of ridicule is overt restlessness, which may lead to floods, to follow nothing but devastation.

Doctor, during this separation from you I had been analyzing the facts and I seem to have grown wiser. I have seen fire and smoke, rather I seem to have known the world. I have seen stillness of flowing rivers and I have seen the movements of desert storms too and I know when the reverse happens people also get upset and even follow suit in reverse orders. These so- called rulers, corrupt politicians and handlers of stirrups of the people, where they were yesterday and what they were earlier is known to me.

I feel volcanoes are erupting within me and in my thoughts and my feelings, even the deer who wander in the plateaus are now seemingly anxious and worried and a statue is covered by a mountain, such are the question which are rising in my mind. There seems to be an enemy within my circles of friends and there is friend waiting among my enemies and years and years of traditional values are getting broken, but I was not defeated, as I fane not left any hope to be rescued out of these adverse circumstances. I was about to open my lips to utter a reply that this period changed the topic all together.

This was the deliberation of my interests in you that I might have become intense and exceeded certain limits, but I don't mean to be discrete or sarcastic and I know the reality of your circumstances, my obligation is to follow your orders only and that too, religiously. I should not resent or complain. You have never sustained or over-ruled my objections and that is enough of an encouragement for me to continue. But you did it at times, your advices had an orderly rule hidden behind their interception. You may not or you may be just trying to interact an advisory role, but at times I do get confused and that maybe because we didn't have a prolonged time of companionship together. You left me confused within a very short time.

This maybe my height of the limit of interest in you that I feel if I take a step in your direction, I will find my destination clearly seen. Our separation had its own toll on me, that I sometimes feels penalized and I rest assure myself that I would get my dreams fulfilled one time, but the thing which I lost was what exactly? I used to break toys in my childhood, I think that is the result of by beginnings. I used to think to whatever item I touch it would turn into gold, but after getting acquainted with you I realized that it was insane thinking.

Yesterday where there was only a wall, today there is a house erected over it, as development don't have to take time to materialize. A swimmer seems to be floating in the pool of water very calmly, but the intricate movements of the limbs would speak for themselves. Whom you left was a different person, and now come back and look over me and you will see a different person holding paramount emotions quietly kept within myself. I used to think I could get everything in the world but in reality, I have to search for something better.

It looks that cities and cities are engulfing the smoke, which is curling up high in the space, even the sky appears to me as a grave of some heart-broken human, that every day a fire erupts from it. I know who would let me sit at ease if I get up and walk out on you. It would be like an awful revulsion for me if I go against your directives, which are well meaning for me. Loving you is like lifting a mountain by myself and I rarely find it impossible to shoulder it over my weak body and soul.

I even get an awkward feeling that you married me for the sake of soliciting your word to your family, but you have soft corners for someone else. How if coolly someone replaces me, I will not be left with any life in me thereafter. I feel like tearing my clothes off in shreds, but I am also afraid who would stich them back for me to wear it, if I go

47

wrong in my assumptions. It looks I have been ripped apart by own absurd thoughts and next day I woke up and awakened with the morning breeze, which could not give me any solace. My God, keep my thoughts under control and do not let them wander in the rough land that sometime later I get sore feet and wait for healing process to begin. I keep garden of my imaginations for you shut, for I don't know if they get burnt and the wind will only scatter the ashes around. After I am gone in non-existence and if you come to visit my place, you may be compelled to do justice with your acts and deeds afterwards.

Yours lovingly.
Being awaited.

SATISFIED DIS-SATISFACTION

Doctor, my dear,

Of late I am getting un-named wishes and I feel I may not get to know them, I am getting un-identified dreams and I feel I may not get their interpretation. Even if my desires boil in my heart I keep silence, there is some kind of helplessness prevailing within me. Sum and moon seem to have developed intimacy with each other and I feel my wants are for your looks I may not get. This sky is meeting both the days and nights and the distances between my days and nights are still far-fetched. Monsoons are coming and going and so also other weathers, but for me I remained exposed to harsh heat. For me these seasons are innocent onlookers of my grief and my thoughts are racing towards you, which you can't see.

To me I am surrounded by a space of isolation, in which I could only see your shadows of quivering whispers, but for others buds are blossoming to spread fragrance of joy. I feel somewhere nearby your senses are attending to me, in your scent of burning desires for me. Far away at the horizon I could see sparkling dew and your tender gaze falling upon me as a protection from pain and sorrow. I feel as if you have touched my heart's cheeks with embalming smoothness' and to me it appears, as if the separation is coming to an end. The harshness of days are getting over and the calmness of cool nights are trying to let me sleep in tranquility.

I don't know why since late evening I am feeling wetness in my eyes and again I am missing you desperately. I want get buried in your imaginations and my sight also had stood still for the same. Time never stays quite as it has to move and time has to pass, it also has the same properties of my thoughts. The fragrance has been set and spread everywhere but you were not around and for me everything got delayed.

I sometime wonder why I don't get friendly with my past friends or someone who did not like me I care no more, it is because you were strange and your glow was strangely attractive for me. The love I had for you was my insanity and this separation is my destiny. I don't have any companion to spend time with, as everyone is busy completing their responsibilities. I have no face in front of me to read and compare with you, as there is no one so close to my heart like you.

Why don't you give me your worries, torment, agony and anguish even if you are feeling deprivations like me, give them all to me and feel better for yourself. I know I may not be capable of lodging those burdens all by myself, let us try and pass on these sufferings to me to share with you, for I see no harm in it. Your suffering cannot be different than mine. Let me see how this world could tease you, and some time let me be your guardian to check all these untoward effects of the world. I don't want to let you share your grievances with others, when I am available for you at all times.

Who says that love needs a language to express, this reality is made obvious by the eyes only, I have registered it very well. People come to explain me, but if I would have had solace in destiny I would not have been so restless, as I am. I have loved you like a life and apologetically you are so away from my life in which I am living day to day. Who would have known that this way it would be? I would be obliged to wait for our union, and you seem to be hiding like a moon behind the clouds. You have made me thirsty of your wants and it appears if you were teasing me for the sake of us only. We have met and separated, how do you expect me to sleep at ease and now I just feel like crying all nights remembering you.

You remember when you lifted my veil, how shy I became in exposing myself. I have now grown up and shyness has overcome the longingness for you. I get dozed off in the small hours of the morning and ask angels to avoid waking me up, as I mostly would be dreaming about you. You appear to be indifferent towards my emotions, and I feel it is better if you extinguish me completely instead of being indifferent.

Yours loving partner

Wall Clock hours seem to have stopped. Time was stalled and made a still portrait of my feelings. I was not able to think clearly and pages of my diary remained blank for some time. I received Doctor's letter and was rejuvenated by freshness and glamour. I wrote.

My dearest,

How nice and considerate of you to have mentioned your busy schedule and your increasing responsibilities towards your work assignments. No doubt your message was delayed and, in my books delayed for long, at least in the end it came and thanks God for the same.

Horizons, rainbows which come and go, moon lighting peeping through clouds, breezes which flow brushing past my face, stars which glitter in the sky, lightening which strikes occasionally and the dark mountains which are seen in the background, all are waiting for you and waiting for me to join you but I only wish I could grasp it and hold it with me forever.

It is not that I am speaking hear-say evidence, I have experienced it myself that flowers bloom out of fire, if your charm is turned into glory and they all for me, are like log fire which I feel like touching and burning my finger-tips. It is all un-true that history repeats itself over time, in which case let it bring back my memories of our time spent in togetherness.

I need to differentiate between ignorance and helplessness, what else I could have done for you if I was heart-broken and had fallen head over heels in love of you, but good thing was hope, which still lingered on and did not disappoint me, no doubt I was getting little apprehensive and anxious too.

My heart is applying to you to call me and listen to my heart beat which is speaking for itself, you are my story and my measure of happiness, you are my habit and my worship, you are my destination and goal, so, forget any indifference cropped due to this separation and come back in response to my applications in continuity.

My feelings are enriched with my blood-stained thoughts and have encrypted on their signs a picture of modest and humble love from a wife and I hope and pray that this picture doesn't change even if the period keep changing its colors, seasons keep changing their landscapes and people keep changing their opinions about me. It is even more challenging for me to think that you are unhappy with the circumstances and this doesn't let my heart to rest in peace.

Hope to see you soon, rather hope to meet you soon.

Yours loveable life partner.

Some more time lapsed and I was feeling better. Even I was getting preoccupied in the routine. I recollected a hint which you gave in your last letter, which I recollected later and thought of enquiring.

Doctor,

I am not sure but I presume you referred to someone in your last latter, someone I didn't know, but I felt there was some ambiguous reference to someone. It may be nothing but if it is I better know and get prepared for. I am sure your commitment is not questioned and neither your sincerity, but why I am getting a feeling that there is someone involved. Someone who may interfere in our lives, someone whom you didn't want to be exhibited.

I am asking myself you are an honest man and you may not have intended to express it, but somehow, I got a reference that there is somebody existing in your letter. I thought of showing your letter to all wise men and women to see and search the non-existent existence of some reference, who is this person and whose work is this. Or I may be getting deluded, I don't know.

I know you will remain faithful, I know you are trustworthy, I know you will even listen to me and you will maintain our relations to the testimony you gave to God for this bond and would tell the truth.

Tell me can you recollect whose reference was there in your letter. Who was mentioned in that letter or who was actually verbalized in that letter.

I am engrossed in this question day and night, being occupied my un-liked and uncalled for suspicions about the reference you un-intentionally made, so much time has passed and as though an era has passed but I am still thinking about the reference, as to whom you were referring in your letter. All may agree that it could be a product of my prolonged and tireless waiting, I am complaining on no grounds and I have no reason to and I am a bit apprehensive about the outcome of all this chaos, but I still need to know who was being wished and blessed in that reference.

The rest is your conscious and your guilt and your responsibility and your confession.

Yours forever

No sooner I wrote this letter I repented for my paranoid ideation. I thought I need not show my letters to the Doctor. He doesn't know I have even filled some pages of my diary for him, but if it was for him he need to know the facts. I thought of tearing off few pages, but he would know that pages were torn. I left them as they are. His reply was brief and self-explanatory. I got convinced and got intimidated by F.A. Faiz and I wrote.

Oh! My partner, my soulmate,

My thoughts are being let out for the sake of inscription meant for catharsis, as you say is mandatory for normal emotions. Your companionship is like the description of Jesus and your honesty is like the chastity of Mariam. My heart and life are devoted for you, and sometime you would know, if not now. I need not worry. Even if you would have had some references, they were talk of the past. Past is past. One cannot live in past, but one can recollect past for the learning sake only.

My whole existence is meant for your consolation and relief, my days are meant for your service and my nights for your solace. What all you would hear about me would be in appraisal of your association and what ever rumors you would be encountered with will point to you and no one else. These are just traditions that needed to be followed and it would become evident that I live for you and I die for you.

Your looks are springs to me and your appearance is my interest in nature, in appreciation of their beauty and glamor. When we will meet my strands of curls will be speaking for themselves, my lips will tell themselves and my eyes would narrate themselves. I envy your confidence and your pretense is on purpose. Your affection is worship worthy and yours be-spectacled stares very meaningful.

Whenever I would come close to you, I would be proud of my gains and my conferences, the walk ways are dusting off with your allure and the breezes which touch you pass on are aromatic of your fondness and your manner of speech is like a speech showered by consolatory idioms', and my waiting will never go in vain and I would get compensatory intensity to remain with you, never to get separated.

Your eyes hide millions of merry gestures and your approach is rewarding of the paradise one could desire upon life to be spent in. Your kindness is intoxicating and force me to think of the calmness after a lightening thunderstorm. Your swaying gait is an understatement of your comfort I could derive by encircling your body and soul.

I can compensate dooms day for your closeness and your strength of arms can compensate for the shivering of my faith in your integrity. I can compensate my shyness for the sympathy you lodge in your eyes and my lips will never tire to talk in your favor. You are like a freshly lighted candle, upon whose glow I could spend days and nights and when we will meet, the morning breezes will turn their directions and the moon will hide behind the clouds.

The gathering of your company should continue forever, let me fall or stumble or hold you for the grip of firmness and the warmth of your embrace. All this is as though a dream for me in which I fell the dampness of dew and coolness of shaded trees. My eyes will blink back tears and my heart will engulf the smoke which it emanates. I will have the control of this world then and I may wish to turn the desert storm into a valley of garden. I may desire for flowers to bloom upon your steps and upon your flips of finger I would change the seasons. Your freshness will be endowed with permanency and your separation a transient affair.

Yours lovingly.

I think I should seek counsel from the elders. But before I seek I should hold trust in people from whom I am seeking advices. I need not seek advice from several people because they will say what they experience and each one may differ in their own perspective of what is right and what is not. I must find a goal in life and then pursue to achieve it. I could not achieve any thing without a pre-formed goal. I can have multiple goals and I can show efforts in the pursuit of my goals.

I was getting wiser with time. In company or without company of Doctor. He is a blessing for me but I am also a blessing for him. I would get as much from him as he would get from me. We were made for each other and that is important. I was told that Doctor was married before me to one lady and this was hearsay evidence, if at all it is true. I believe my father had requested Doctor not to disclose it before me. He said she need not know. The interesting fact is Doctor kept to his words and we never brought that topic in discussion all our lives.

IMPERFECT 6 TEMPTATIONS

This intimidating environment surrounding my future enveloped by mist of cold intermittent outbursts of hostilities was actually waiting for me to intercept them and not allowed to be blown out of proportions. Stories made up and spiced to hammer my mind, giving intolerable pain, excruciating discomfort, exploding my already shattered confidence were acting as last nail in the coffin.

If my blurred orientation to the mishaps were anywhere accurate, it left no help to regain this set in which an execution of trappers exonerated over our family to spring then shut, shut in totality was breaking the required trust in any relationship. Doctor's statements of effective strategy behind his suffering more so by his own will and wish was beyond my understanding and seemed nothing but a maddening wall with many breaks.

The journey was long. There were no direct flights from my home town to North Africa. We were obliged to change once at the international airport in the sub-continent itself and we have to take many hours of transit in Europe, depending upon the carrier, either in Rome, or in Athens or in Istanbul, or somewhere. Good thing was there were senior frequent traveler's family with me and I knew Doctor would be there waiting for me. I was not ready to face him. I was not mentally prepared for this union and I was not sure how that strange thing, it would turn out to be.

We also admitted our defenseless obsolesces about the current issues on presumed announcements thereafter to convert the so-called values into normalcy. We were allowed to interact the way it suited you, but perils got included and confronted my limits. It was strange but acceptable not on the basis that it would have continued without an end and unexpected mishaps got connected with the routine. I found it not easy to touch on this very crucial and relevant topic and could not confide in anyone who could be vaguely aware of this situation. Doctor also expressed the confusion about the difficulties associated with disclosures too.

I opened the bag of letters exchanged during this time of separation and they appeared to be new and unread, in spite of me having read them several times. I had written to Doctor not to leave me behind. I wrote: it seemed to be as if you just came and left. You couldn't have reached me fully and I had not explored you fully well. You shadowed like a spring with blossomed flowers which underwent a calamity and vanished. You could just pledge me with your fragrance of striking incense added with the flavors of young buds, yet to be sprinkled with the colors of rainbow.

There was no time left for the breeze to get fulfilled with your aroma and my gazes continued wandering to get astray, the boundaries not to be crossed. There was no time for the gray evening to pass on to dusk and to mix with the night and my palpitating heart couldn't seek any rest and peace. Let me live a moment longer in your imaginations, your portrayed images and your shadows. Let me gulp down the intoxicating feeling for your admiration and mist and love. We could exchange any words and you didn't utter a word in appreciation of my person, thirsty with desires for you. I could see stars twinkling in the sky, glittering like uncut diamonds and candles are lighted at home for your presence and their yellowish glow is seeping in the space around me.

Doctor wrote back in so many words:

Now don't interrupt me or my thoughts, feelings, obligations and duties, neither step in front of me to stop my moves, my paths, my ways and my directives. If I would have stayed back, I would never have been able to leave you and could have gone ahead to undertake the tasks and hurdles which I needed to cross, the social bindings which I had to overcome and the pending challenges which I had to settle. You would have continued demanding my presence and I would have stayed back, which I shouldn't have done and couldn't have afforded. These requirements and obsessions would never have ended. This was not a succession which you could have win over and get rewarded for.

I was amazed by his short but lovable and reasonable reply and wrote:

I can't complain, but you left me quickly with incompleteness of my whims and fancies, with my unfulfilled wishes and desires, and I was living with incomprehensible apprehensions about you.

My thirst and hunger were not quenched but I compromised with the realities of life, yours and mine. In our walks of life such dimensions would arise and test my patience, I never thought. I am afraid if there would be ongoing stations of such tests and trials yet to be faced and warranting longingness for each other and the unsatisfied solaces for each other. It is not an anxious thought, it is my stamped affection for you.

Doctor was prompt and he wrote briefly, may be because of paucity of time:

I can't live without you either, even the mere thought of it is killing for me, I myself had not relinquished my desires for you and it will remain only for a transient time, we have faced the tragic separation but union is waiting at the corner for us to compensate for it.

I resisted my urge not to document these feelings but I wrote back:

In time od joys and sorrows, for the inevitable destiny of written happiness and sadness, which we tasted are encountered by many more like us and faced by all at some time or the other. If we get defeated how will we survive the merriness and gloom which we are supposed to share, the difficulties and conflicts so common of times, we will share and live, live and share.

You may continue trying on me and you may do so any number of times, but also find time to look into my eyes, my mortal soul is already dedicated for you. It will remain so and I will not let you feel the difference of real and virtual. Who is around in this transient world for me to listen, except your listening ears. I had never tasted the grief of separation before and this grief got delayed and I swear upon your adoration that your sorrows are my sorrows.

You feel free to speak out your feelings and don't remain silent, you may confide your fears and anxieties surrounding you. If you don't spell out then with whom you could share. I am not a stranger and not unknown to you. Your acquaintance had made me make believe and induce a faith of totality and you are no more a disjointed part of me. I am not distanced and live with in you.

I was surprised. How is it possible? There were two unopened letters from Doctor. How could I miss them? How on earth this could happen? I hurriedly opened them and they were addressed to me. Doctor wrote:

There are heartless people, even stone hearted, but let them know that I have written some poetic verses for you. You have been writing captive verses for me, now I intend to write poetry describing your prettiness and your grasping attractiveness, which only I have seen and me alone could describe. I feel compelled to write poetry for you, I have become poet for you and writing poetry in your praise, your admiration and your exquisiteness. I have become an unknown un-named poet for you.

I could write any number of couplets for you, in your favor and just for you. I am your critic and I am your cherisher. I could submit to any number of years recollecting and endorsing my adoration and lasting impressions of your glow of innocence, shine of radiant color, tantalizing sparkle of your eyes and glitter of incredibly grasping image. I am also waiting for you, as eager as you are waiting for lineage towards me.

Your eyes are worship worthy, your curves of eyebrows praise worthy, the light in your glances are seductive and the smile an invitation which no one could refuse. Your face a beauty for ever for me. All these images are imprinted in the folds of my memory that I can not even forget your casted shadows which reflected your body contours. I am yielding to you and could continue doing to as long as l can.

I realize I should become a saint and leave this world, for the courage it demands and get dissolved in the surroundings full of your presence, emanating your fragrance around and get lost in search for you. But I failed and failed miserably, as you were everywhere. The forests were yours, the rivers were yours, the mountains were yours and the valleys were yours. The entire world belonged to you so, anywhere I go I will get lost and would be forced to return home and wait for you.

Some night, some dark night was lighted by moon, full moon's bluish fluorescent light was glowing in the city streets. All people looking at the moon were discussing about you. Your moon-faced beauty was compared and your grace was talked about. Some said it was your mesmerized face which is glowing up high in the sky. I was there keeping quite astounded by people's versions. I couldn't have confided in them. I was becoming increasingly unsure of myself, and my relationship with you.

I had to leave, I couldn't dare talk to anyone, every one was occupied by your images and talks. At that moment I felt crazy to seek your attention and felt mad to go insane. Beyond doubt it was my fault. My insane sanity or sane insanity that I felt I am to be blamed and me alone, even there was no obvious fault of mine. I remained tightlipped and I remained silent, not verbalizing a word about you, for fear of your defamation. I feel I need rehabilitation to recover form your love. You became the cause of it and you become the remedy for me.

Even my presence was noticed, people asked me about you, all referred you to me and all made enquiries about you. I kept quiet, smiling within myself with no expression people could interpret from it, I maintained silence to avoid slander. I can't imagine people slandering about you, I could do anything to hide your identity. The purpose was to keep the eventuality.

The journey ended without any untoward events, the accompanied family was of big help. I liked the interim transit but it was expected for me to find every thing strange. I was preoccupied by the prospects of reaching Doctor. I was even afraid whether he would recognize me after a long separation, especially when we had not exchanged the recent photos of each other. But Doctor's features were engraved in my mind and I expected not a big change in him. Our plane landed and we had to walk the tarmac to get to the visitors awaiting reception. I located Doctor from a distance and practically ran and embraced him. Embraces were not the part of culture of that country and I held him tightly for a long time, until he gestured the lady accompaniment who rescued as she understood the newly weds long lasting separation and this much awaited meeting. She consoled me and we got into the car.

It was evening time and the Mediterranean weather was getting very cool, almost touching my skin, as I was wearing tropical clothes. Doctor handed over his jacket to me and helped me to put it over my shoulders. It was a good feeling to be covered by his warm jacket. The scent he wears was so pleasant and the surroundings were so green. There was no conversation during the ride back to his home, now our home. From distance we could see the massive collection of prefabricated housing blocks, put together and housed all or most of the expatriates from different countries, who came here to work.

Doctor had friend to lift my luggage and by the time we reached home and climbed third floor, it was getting dark. Curiously I was not feeling tired and the common area lights were switched on. We entered and lighted our new home. I was amazed by the clean and elaborate rooming capacity and the decent furnishing Doctor has decorated inside. He started introducing me the drawing room the small passage, the living room with adjacent neat kitchen will all found, and at the end of the apartment was our bedroom, a storage room with a closet, and of course there were two bath rooms. One attached to our bed room. All looked so elegant and nice.

He showed me how to operate the taps for sink and tub. It was not like back home. Every thing was modern and eastern European style. There was supply of cold and hot water and shampoos, soaps, tooth brushes and tooth paste all arranged at their appropriate places. I immediately felt like getting a bath and get fresh. I told him and he passed on the bath robe then and my clothes bag to be carried inside. He knew my shyness and he was considerate. He helped me to fill the tub with Luke warm water and poured some foaming solution for bathing. I waited until he closed the door, as though he is a stranger, but I will get used to intimacies their after.

I came out with dribbling water from my hair and he helped me to dry my hair with a towel. By that time food was arranged on the dining table and I felt hungry smelling the aroma of cuisines he has made. I ate and felt sleepy and slept well. All night and next day I was awakened by the morning sun rays filtering through nylon curtains and spreading over our bed. His side of bed was creaseless, which made me understand that he has not slept last night. Probably he didn't want to disturb me. He was looking fresh even otherwise. Next day was his weekly off and we had all the time in the world.

His friends and neighbors started dropping as they wanted to see the not so new bride. I was wearing casual dress and they did not mind it. We had small talk and exchanged pleasantries. Most of his friends belonged to our home town and they were good people. I never felt any strangeness among them. We almost became friends and I was participating in talks as though I knew them since long. Some of our in-laws were acquainted with these people and we had a lot of women's chatter.

Doctor served them cool drinks and roasted dry fruits. Time passed so quickly and I did not realize that it is almost noon time and I have to look into refrigerator for food or cook some for us. The guests left and we were together again. All by ourselves and so much of privacy at our disposal. We had no one to answer and no one to attend. We had all the time in the world to exchange our own feelings. Doctor held my hand and took me to bed room and all the expected sequelae of this separation were met with. We were so much satisfied that I felt like sleeping again, which Doctor did not permit for me to get over the time lag.

He showed me the local currency, the American dollars, and taught me the exchange values of each. That time the local Dinar was almost one hundred and twenty rupees of our subcontinent and each dinar could fetch an equant of 3.3. dollars. All these were not understandable for me but I kept listening to his explanations. We kept things which I brought from home at appropriate places and he taught me operation of stove and showed me the necessary eatables in the frig. We could have called it a day.

INTERNALIZING 7 EVIDENCES

My home assignments coupled with my other pre-occupations should have kept me busy to while away some time, instead I forced myself to be carried to horizons of mist of confusion over other matters and I thought of seeking some reassurance and solace. In the mean time I lamented my loss of time and intercepted my wisdom over my obvious suffering. I knew it was important not to deviate from the goals, leave alone the hurdles and then relevant roamed around irrelevancies not making any turns towards the relevant. References made out of non-existent sources become covert strategic procedures and they bring bout obvious understandable solutions, and our own perceptions become important in the end. How our own perceived things direct us to become narrow or broad minded, but in the end it all jots down to individuals' reactivity and nothing matters thereafter.

I was underweight, in spite of my 'hour glass' shape and Doctor wanted me to gain weight. He advised me that weight has to be in comparison to height. I was tall as per south Asian standards and I should put on some weight. He asked me to remind him to get certain things when we will go out shopping. I expected markets full of shops and restaurants. It turned out to single store large building clumped with all utilities from electronics to vegetables. Some racks were empty, revealing that certain shipments are being awaited. I believe everything depends on shipments. Huge cargo ships would be waiting at the dockyard to be unloaded.

He took me in his beetle Volkswagen and showed me places. People were of mixed colors, both whites and blacks. Whites were dressed like Europeans and blacks were from the southern desert dressed in traditional clothes. Women folk did not wear veils, instead they are covered by shawls depending upon the weather conditions. There was a cold indifference between foreigners and the locals. I believe locals were paid less than foreigners and naturally they would consider them as rivals. But locals had many other privileges, which they don't consider at hand.

The weather was cool and comfortable, the sun was warm but not harsh. The roads were clean but not very wide. The houses were similar looking and rested against each other. I could understand why I was missing ceiling fans in our home. The climate was never too hot to need fans. Instead there were heaters to be occasionally used in winters. The doors and windows were air-tight for the reason of occasional desert storms which may invade the city and in spite of being air-tight, there will be fine powdered sand which would get sprinkled on the furniture and floor, I was told by Doctor. I was preoccupied by the need to inform our families of my safe reaching.

We stopped at the telegraph office, as there was no phone facility at homes for security reasons, I believe. The leader was cautious about mutiny and rebellion or revolt or even civil war. But he was a handsome man and I liked his manner of speech and his presentable mannerisms. He was mostly seen on TV and mostly among some familiar faces, whom I didn't recognize neither was interested in knowing. There were few people and many cubicles. We need to register where we are calling and allocated a numbered cubicle and supposed to wait, until indicated. We were connected to home town and I spoke at length, without noticing Doctor's restlessness on my small talk. Later he told me that we were charged in conversion to homeland currency a bill of seven hundred rupees, equivalent to a monthly phone bill back home.

I could never understand numbers, accounts, bills and economics. But I should learn and I have to be a Roman in Rome, as the saying goes. Nevertheless, I was happy that a promise was met with and people must be rest assured of my safe landing in safe hands. A formality was over. I also knew that it is better to use telephone for important and brief communication, otherwise there was the facility of letter postage, to go into details. We went to city center, which as the old city, very similar of Lord's Bazar, with cramped shops and smaller lanes only to walk through. I was astonished when we reached the clothes market of small shops with bundles of glamorous cloths, labelled Dinar ½, 1 and 1 ½ only per meter. So cheap and so gaudy. Velvets, chiffons, embroidered satins and what not. I was tempted but Doctor again converted the exchange value and also informed me that there are no tailors available for stitching.

I froze completely when we approached the Gold market. Shops were overflowing with gold ornaments, not be-jeweled but little crude, all glittering in the lights of the shops, almost exposed to touch. I stood back and wondered, who would need to wear so much of gold. Doctor notified that ladies are crazy about it and would only show off when they remove their shawls. It is a sign of prestige and position. I didn't care, but I thought a photo of mine with the background of this kind would be a pleasant surprise of people back home. Doctor happily complied to my request, because it did not warrant spending money. He was a couscous man.

It was getting late, I was hungry and it was lunch time. We returned home, warmed the food from the frig and felt drowsy. We slept till late afternoon. He took me out to introduce me to his neighbors and friends. Most of them were from the divided sub-continent and had migrated to our neighbor country. They were sweet and cordial. I was wearing my white Sari and jeweled neck collar with matching ear rings. All praised my looks and we all became acquainted to become friends thereafter. All wives had a common problem to while away the time while their husbands were gone to work. All used to assemble down in the parking lot and make programs to pass time with fun and frolics.

I immediately liked the surrounding and the construction of housing colony and collection of same language speaking crowd in one place. It was a community of its own with common interests and common aims. They were all humble and soft spoken. They liked me and I liked them. Even otherwise Doctor would give some assignments for me to pass time while he is away and everything became so easy for me. He had a knack of keeping me busy. He thought I would not miss my people. As such I was not missing them. There was so much to do and so much to remain occupied with.

The problem arose when Doctor was called in the nights to see patients. Ambulances were sent on specified roster days and he was obliged to attend them. Some places were distantly placed and he would take a long time to return. I expressed my fear of loneliness and since then he started carrying me with in the ambulance. I used to sit in the ambulance and he would attend and return. Rarely he would leave me in company of old gatekeepers, who would offer bread and watermelon to me, a strange combination to eat. In spite of not able to understand their language and slang I had good time with their laughs and talks. They were good people and understood my presence among them.

The real problem arose when he was posted for night duty for the whole night in rotation. I couldn't have gone with him to the hospital. It was not allowed. I remained sleepless worried for nothing. Then he managed to get me enough cassettes of home country's local films to watch, gave additional assignments for special time-consuming deserts to be made and sweaters to be knitted for no obvious need. I was supposed to pass time and I did and even got used to it, with passage of time. He would request his fiend's wives to visit after he was gone to while away some more time. He was a considerate man.

Later he carried me to his foreigner friends who were working with him, from eastern Europe and Philippines. The male Doctor from Poland was a sweet old man with two grown up daughters. He started calling me 'Princess', probably because of the way I used to dress. He must have seen Princesses wearing such jeweled necklaces and bracelets. They served us their own special preparations. His wife was also a working member and spoke with kind gestures and Doctor used to translate. The process was very interesting and even little bit jocular and we all laughed whole heartedly. Their daughters were reserved like most of the European girls and it did not make a big difference.

The meetings of house-wives downstairs were useful as I collected bits and pieces of information from all senior residents about the working conditions of this place. The formalities of coming are easier but the formalities of going were tedious. You have to get clearances from several departments of 'No objections' before you can get your exit and re-entry endorsed on your passport to allow you to purchase ticket for home country. I believe, one very senior Doctor, who is here for several years, whose children were studying here just couldn't develop enough courage to undergo the formalities of exit and stayed back.

One unemployed person living with his family was happier than employment back home. Well there are always interesting characters to be found everywhere. Only two things were prohibited one being to avoid talking about the leader in public and second to bring magazines from outside. Liquor was banned but foreigners accustomed to drinking knew how to brew their own liquors and managed to resume their lifestyles and continued with making their stay in comfort.

When Doctor used to return from night duty he would bring fresh bacon and butter and fry the slices and serve me with orange juice at the bed, while I was asleep. He brought Cadbury's chocolates, my weakness and mango juice canned from some south American country which tasted like home grown mangoes and I used them plenty. I was gaining weight. The commodities dependent on shipments were stacked when arrived and sometimes, things like bulbs, shirts, tires and other accessories were all of a sudden available in plenty. Next day all will have bulbs in their houses brightly lit, all cars will have new tires and everyone is seen wearing same type of shirts.

The ladies club of the block notified the norms of this place and the norms of the husbands of this place that they want their wives to be presentable, their houses presentable, to be attired in negligee while welcoming them, husbands returning from work, wait on them for 15 minutes before speaking out, have a meal prepared warm and served on the table and to sit beside them looking at their faces, remain on negligee for the rest of the afternoon until some guests arrive or till night time, moving around in the silhouettes of the window light and watch TV programs with their husbands and sleep together.

What a non-sense? Does husbands think wives have no hearts, no brains and no stomachs? Doctor may become one like them in a short time and would prefer the same routine even on weekends. As though I am a soldier living in a war zone and ongoing war is on women. It seems to be a real war and an ugly war. Why can't there be pillow fights, hide and seek games involved here. Women should be strong, they should depend on strong supporting structures, strong resources, strong political contacts or whatever. They have to protest.

They have to be fearless, because it is the fear of consequence or repercussions, which makes them weak. More importantly they have to be assertive, not submissive or passive-aggressive. They have to be just firm, and stern and put the foots down and ask for their rights. They should know first and teach their husbands later that both genders are equal but not identical. At least they must pretend to be powerful, as power understands power and cruelty understands cruelty. They should be ambassadors of women's empowerment, even if they have law degrees with them or not. Women need not be anatomy only, they should be physiology also. They should teach that being receptive doesn't mean women are foolish.

Without women, the mankind would get endangered and then will become extinct and so they have the legacy to remain sustainer of mankind with the grace of God. They should stop getting perpetuated by any abuse. They should allow to be talked over, they should make themselves heard, listened and allowed speech as and when they want. No doubt with freedom of speech, they should not go on and on like a typical day's laborer's work schedule. They need not be chief justices, members of legislative assembly or senate.

They shouldn't be allowed any discrimination based on sex or gender. They must get the 1st and 2nd amendments of American constitution and show their husbands, even if they do not know the constitution itself. They need not get involved in conflict of interests, they should as well be mediators or pacifiers or moderators or something of some kind. They need not make a hell out of nothing, as they have to make heaven in homes. They need not be contestants of beauty pageants or popularity contests, because in contests someone has to win and someone has to lose. They also better get prepared for failure, as failures teach more lessons than success.

They need not be lesser evils or lesser gods, they can remain humble, subtle, modest and simple and still can win. There are other weapons they have which they can use in times of need. They should be understood by others and not misunderstood. I mean mankind or men folks. They need not depend on TV screens, or theatrical shows to put up with women. This was what Doctor has told me and I don't know if he would deny it later. Women should not forget even if they forgive. They have better biological instincts to remain living, definitely better than men.

They should not be iconic figure to be touched but not felt. They should be humanly humane and should also know the statutes of limitations. They should not wait too long to let the men get accustomed to abuse, they must raise their voice, protest or even can migrate. Migrate to some shelter for a day or two, longer times may allow husbands to forget them and get involved with others. As we have our own competitors. Men should be their original selves, they need not be saints or predators.

INTIMIDATING 8 TRIVIALITIES

With information missing, what was learned, what was classified, what was the point in the first place was nothing to comprehend. Nothing except a despairing sense of ineffectuality mingled with distortions. The commotion was given so much importance, so much attention that there was nothing left for negotiations and nothing faintly hopeful of reconciliations in this, warranting caution.

Old and recent memories started surfacing in my mind and I recalled how thoroughly knowingly he was influencing my mind with punctures of doubts, suspicions untraceable to their origins. My mind set towards the game of power and control was to subjugate his relationship to my satisfaction actually Tanta mounting to nothing short of abuse, which I was not aware of initially.

With regards to problems they can be purchased, displayed, displaced, ignored, solved, attended and overcome. I should not let the world know that I am easily prone to become nervous wreck, because what we see is usually what we wanted to see. We are although not expected to do what is expected out of us, rather we should do what we want to do. Doctor may note that he could learn any more or any less or very little that is valuable but register that in any case, recesses have to be filled for clear coverage of distant past and clear sailing for distant future. Accepting the ground reality remains, and what remains to be done is accepting our positions, different family origins and of course arrogances of exertions.

I always wanted Doctor to dress well. He wanted to mix with haggard looking locals. Over grown hair, no matching clothes and casual looks. He looked good even otherwise but I wanted him to look better. I purchased a high collar shirt, a tie, a hat and a coat. 'Oh! This damn thing of my asphyxiating tie over a high collar shirt biting my neck, this stuffed cat collar making me feel a prey for any predator to attack and tight brimmed hat causing headache. Oh! It is killing me. I better take them out and go back to my loosely fitting trousers, oversized shirts and a silken scarf to go along with all that, so comfortable'. Doctor was talking to himself, in his shelled fantasies with which he was accustomed.

I sometime feel he has erected a glass shield around him which can't be penetrated to reach him. He may be a mad lunatic or a wise lunatic or disordered personality. To hell with his mental makeup. He removed the newly purchased items and worn his usual clothes. What a waste of money, waste of resources, a waste of livelihood and a waste of survival. But his friends say, in his usual attire and ungroomed hair, he easily gets mixed with the locals and people cannot identify him as a foreigner. With his fluency in Arabic spoken language and the local slang it was difficult to differentiate him from the crowd.

Once one old lady has visited him and explained her story and collected her prescription happily returned and came back asking him is he not a local, and wen he admitted it, she threw her papers and said 'No benefit' in Arabic and left. Later he was given the post of board member along with his senior partner, Polish Doctor. He used to translate and write reports for referred patients from military for their fitness to serve, from court to signify about patient's criminal responsibility and from ministry of external affair to evaluate and asses a patient's free treatment abroad on government expenses.

It was an important position and he was offered money and gifts, which he always refused. Some people came to know his apartment and used to deliver them outside the door, which innocently I used to collect and keep them. I took them as tokens for appreciation of his service. But he knew how hazardous it can become, if matters are reported to authorities. But he happily used to oblige his friends request with his recommendations, without fabricating the diagnosis. He served the medical board for a long time and did not exploit his position, while I was enjoying the free gifts and free accessories which were not easily available in the market.

Trips to nearby towns and cities were enjoyable. The beach was not too far, as we were located on the coast of Mediterranean Sea and the down town visits were entertaining. Friends used to gather fully equipped with all amenities and gas tanks full to venture outings in individual cars. The high way was clear and long rides, a joy. We would be listening to our favorite songs and chatting across the bypassing cars. There were hill stations and valleys, mountains and forests. The beaches were wonderful. We used to select shady trees to spread matts, chat and eat, tell stories and crack jokes. It was so trilling for me, at least.

One day Doctor was in a serious mood and kept his reserve.

'Is there anything I can do', was my question. He lifted his eyebrows looked at me and was seen mumbling. I cannot depend on helpless factors, helpless as cows who are being milked, helpless as infants whose nappies needed to be changed, helpless as deer caught among wolves.

'Just keep cool', was my answer. I know he gets into such moods at times.

'Can you explain'?

'What is there to explain'. I can make a living, a living out of a living and I have my own bucket to kickoff in times of needs, or deeds or mis-deeds.'

I was asking him a straight question and expecting a straight answer, not from others but from him. I am not a janitor or a loser. I am myself and can become a useful one too. Given time, given chance, given support, given evidence, given facts, given truth. I can even be an author. But who would read my book, who would take the trouble to go to a bookstore and purchase my book, who would be interested in characters of my book. There is no illustration, no pictures, some story untold for some time. I should not bother to print it. I should just keep it like my diary in a trunk and lock it.

This is vanity, vanity which is hidden, vanity of backstage and vanity which others expect out of me. Doctor infects his mood on me. It is not about talent, art or craft, intelligence, experience, wisdom or truth. Some recollections to be recollected and narrated. I don't want to be a part of it. Any part of it. I am better off without my story. I am good as I am. Now or in the past or I the future. Moreover, I don't have many impressions in my memory. My memory is fading out, which is patchy and confabulated. It may distract my short term memory too. Long term memory not worthy of narration. What a chaos?

Doctor, you don't understand, you have no idea what it is like. What it should be. What it had been. What it is going to be. I am standing in the spotlight of the stage. Center stage, focused already bright, but I want to be brighter still. All eyes should get focused on me, watching my every move, watching my changing expressions, watching my unlimited non-existent talent. I can't breathe, my mouth is dry. I am dizzy, and I could count my palpitations and my gurgles' in the stomach. I can feel pumping of blood in my head, my legs becoming jelly like, my arms aching and I am feeling light headed and light bodied. I have to speak when it becomes necessary, when it becomes obligatory, when it becomes mandatory, when it becomes compulsory. Now it is compelling.

What is happening to me. My mouth looks gagged, my mind shut, body numb and I am dumb. First, I have to move, I stood up, I staggered and I was in Doctor's arms. There was silence. Total silence. I must have fainted as I fainted on my wedding reception. But Doctor's firm grip worked like decoction and I started feeling better, I felt much better in his arms. How long he could have held me. He slipped me to bed and covered me with a quilt. Oh! God the things which I had been successful were vague and unclear and even distorted. I must turn away from my dark sides, dark secrets, dark fiction, dark ditches of my thoughts, dark ambitions of my feelings. All is false and untrue. I should not ponder about those things anymore.

Listen and look. I shall make myself a Princess, a Queen, Beauty Queen of a Beauty Pageant. What do they know about Shakespeare, what do they know about the feel of gray winter, what do they know about glamorous summer, what do they know about the shriveled autumn or what do they know about blooming colorful spring. No nothing. Their system, their beliefs, their faith and their acts and deeds. Let them go to hell. I shouldn't bother for them. Doctor just gave me a hug. A hug of solace, a hug of an experience which I never experienced before. He was an artist.

I knew if he could have afforded a second-hand harmonica, he would have been a celebrated singer, if he could have afforded a canvas and oil paints, he could have been like Van Gouge, the celebrity painter. One needs basics to depend upon for progress of any talent. Nobody can withstand the truth. Truth has enormous conviction and truth will always win. I better tell the truth than lies. Truth can be tolerated but not stupidity. Tolerance to stupidity is wisdom. In sub-continental cinema at some time 'yodeling' became popular, what the hell is that, a rhyme or a rhythm or a noise, a music or a composition which is a product of non-sense. It is a deviation from norms.

But why am I thinking about all this. The over all routine was all Doctors used to work from 8 am to 2 pm and the rest of the time spending was on their own. Afternoon naps became a habit and evening strolls or visits to friend's houses was yet another routine. There were neighboring country's female spinster nurses who were also given shared accommodation and occasional neighbor was from Arab country, who didn't mix with the others for language barriers. The adjacent block had mechanics, young bachelor boys from neighbor country and they used to do small favors for meal or snack with families. Both the groups were allowed entry in our home and both groups liked me. They would come for a home-made food and cup of tea and would spend a lot of time chatting with us.

There was a constant circuitous flow of expatriates some people leaving and others replacing them. Mixing with locals were minimum, but few locals used to visit Doctor and speak either in Arabic or English. They used to bring gift and eatables and were nice boys, may be recovered patients or students. They took us to their lavish homes are were served Arabic delicacies. Friday used to be the government holiday and we used to go to downtown to sit at the beach or the corridor restaurant for a cup of coffee. Arabic coffee was a popular drink even among foreigners, as they couldn't help get any other drink. The cemented flat railing was a favorite spot to sit and watch the waves touching the shore and fading. We could see sea animals like fishes, crabs and corals too.

Time used to pass quickly at the beach. Behind the scene were building of ministries and courts and mosques. There were parks with greeneries and few flower pots kept at the corners accompanied with benches for the visitors to sit. All new model cars were visible moving on roads and some were worn out rusted old models, as the repairs were a big formality. One has to get a police clearance to get the car dents removed. Vendors used to move in jeeps with open backs displaying the goods and merchandise for sale. Pedestrians were few people who would have parked their cars in alleys and preferred walking around. We used to see both whites and blacks and could notice the discrimination of treatment with one another.

TV watching was a forced pass time and leader was mostly speaking about his policies and his antagonism about the west. The country was friendly with east and that is why most of the foreigners were from eastern European countries. Military service was compulsory and youngsters were obliged to get enrolled and used to try all means of escape from enrollment. The deciding factor were reposts given by the Doctors and Doctors were respected for their opinion. There were occasional bearded preachers who were seen on TV and suddenly they used to get vanished from the screens. Doctor used to translate most of the contents, which he found may interest me. There were no commercials or Adds.

Most of the faces seen around the leader were that of some high-ranking officials given different designations but the control was in the hands of the leader himself. Once Doctor took me to a book store which was green, all green, actually filled with racks of some green color bounded books, written by the leader as per his claim and preached his own philosophy of governance. Patriots were supposed to keep a copy of that book on the mantel or central table to show their allegiance to the leader. The leader's body guards were girls belonging to his family, smart, good looking, and elegant, wearing military uniforms and carrying Russian weapons. But all these scenes didn't disturb our life styles. What people were afraid of were emergency exits, upon some complaint and the people had to leave the country within 24 hours. That was the punishment considered by all.

Our lives were spent in comfort. I was referring to the lady's club congregations, we didn't know how stressful our husbands used to find their work schedules. Every one was afraid to commit mistakes or bypass the laws of the land. Our immediate neighbors were from the sub-continent and there was good mixing among both faiths. I was favorite of one senior Doctor's wife who used to advise me on matters of relevance. She used to teach me the methods to please the husbands and was a witty and humorous person. She was white and her husband was black, but they had good understanding and her husband was a thorough gentleman. They had two kids whom she had put on dieting, as they were getting fat.

One of the Doctor's friend was an interesting man. He could not say 'No' to anybody. He would always be trying to please people. Doctor was fond of him and he was fond of Doctor. He would judge what Doctor intend to say and then would support his point of view.

Doctor would say' What a weather'? and he would reply 'What a weather'?

Doctor would add, 'Lousy is it not'? he would add 'Oh! What a lousy weather, I hate this weather, you are right. It is difficult to stretch our stay here'. Doctor would comment,

'No, I am talking about todays weather, but Mediterranean climate is boon to us'.

'Oh! Yes, it is only todays weather, otherwise what a climate of this country. One can live all his life just on account of the climate. Cool and pleasant'.

'What about sand storms?' Doctor would stop at that.

'Yes'. He would also stop.

'Worse'.

'Definitely worse, bad than worse, I don't know how people can get along with sand storms, most unpleasant and most horrific'.

'No, but they are not permanent'.

'Yes, they are only transient, they come and go and do not disturb us. We can manage with them. Rather they are a pleasant change from the routine'.

This is how the conversation would proceed and I used to enjoy these hilarious talks. casual talks, small talks which were very refreshing.

HERD OF ABUSERS

It was not merely exchange of feelings and expression of uncertainties, it was actually buying embarrassments forced on both sides, getting dismissed by hypocrisies' in conversations and word jargon in communications. I am giving myself something to think about, something to introspect, something to get insights of what was going on. I can call it as a parting gift of a well-wisher as I will know now and then I will never subsequently purchase problems in my life. But how could I explain the slow creeping changes in myself, slow deviation from existing norms, slow subjugation of my personality strengths and slow development of uncertainties about my comfort levels.

There are no elements of surprises in my story, but adventures have some risks in it. Credibility has to be relevant than the risks. So, I need not worry or at least not to brood or not to gloom over it. That language you spoke Doctor, you were not with me. I will regret to have heard it sooner or later. At some point of time you told me that you will not leave me again, but now you are planning to leave again. Some justification of studies, exams, some extra qualifications to be decorated with. There will be some plea some where for justification. 'It is across the sea', Doctor told me, as though it is just across the road. But his friends encouraged him and he placed a family with me and left to Europe. I believe he has to go to Austria, England and Ireland.

He left with a small hand carry. He always preferred to travel light. That family was given a room adjacent to ours. They lived their life, mostly indoors or more precisely in their bed room. There were very few interactions and they belonged to our hometown. The husband was black and his wife was white. They had good understanding and mostly spoke in gestures or whispers. I minded my own business. I restarted my routine and at least had some company in absence of company in the house. At least I was not afraid. Doctor can't be followed everywhere. Moreover, he is noble man, but he doesn't see it that way. He and me are two different persons living together. We are in transit about to cross boundaries.

I was getting a terrible feeling. We will have to sit and talk, to understand our values and put together our exchanged promises. One can do extra-ordinary things in an ordinary way and also can do ordinary things in an extra-ordinary away. Well my dear, in strange countries amazing things can happen, more to come and more to go. I think it is warranted that I get into a contract with Doctor, a contract which should remain viable forever, a contract not like a broken dream. Doctor, you need not worry about people, as to what they will question you. They will question me and I am capable of replying to them. Now I am on top with your patronage and your support.

What? You want me to look into other phases of my life. I don't have any. No background, no realities except some fiction which I have preserved for my spare time. I had watched TV commercials, they were master pieces of reality for marketing techniques. They can sell a bald man, hair brushes, hair dyes and hair straighteners. You can interpret chapters of my book as pornographic but they are fictitiously erotic dramas, that happens in real life. Maliciously made fiction for the kick of it. It is what people like to read. I can't help it. I am out of true expression of true self. Nothing bogus and nothing non-fiction. Just a true story of truth. It will turn out into a big or small budget motion picture with academy awards in all categories. I can produce my own movie.

I may arrange some fund raisers to collect sufficient funds for the same. Fund raisers are the in-thing now a days, they make heaps of money by fooling around but I have a purpose. Loyalty towards my goals. Wisdom and stupidity are a dangerous combination. I should gather more spectacular ambitions to feel contented. I am not a whistle but can make my lips to blow a whistle. I can even sing melodies with my whistle. This is a great country of self-made leaders and followers in plenty to follow suit. No body thinks before taking leaps. They may cross or they may fall. They don't bother.

Here people believe in contracts, contracts for business, contracts for work, contracts for dealing but contracts are not good for relationships. One cannot sustain relationships based on contracts. Not with 24 hours daily routine for life. Here people also talk about qualifications. Qualification they are qualified to ask. But I don't have any and I don't want any. To be precise qualifications are of no value, they are just papers made genuine or fake to prove one's skills, but what if skills are acquired from practice and training.

I better get into politics. Politics of this place are interesting they have comedy, thrill and tragedy all mixed with humor. This is life and chances have to be availed. What I need to do is write a good review about 'Green book' and I will become a celebrity. It looks ridiculous but ridiculous is the other name of politics. I can hold the destiny in my lines of my palm. But I had no control over the political changes which were brought in by the leader. Leader's name was not pronounced in public, instead he was referred as 'Big Brother'. His changes of policies were sudden and dramatic. The country was controlled by 'Revolutionary high command', a group of hand few of people who were the only ones authorized to use 'Red' ink. The country was ruled under the fear of being executed under anti-nationalistic tendencies.

One day he announced that the residents of dwelling would become the owners. The following few days were a havoc for submissions of proof of residence and ownership papers were granted to tenants. Overnight rich became poor and vice versa. One day he de-monetized the currency to take out hoarding of 'Black money', and the following few days witnessed another havoc when queues were standing in front of banks to convert limited money exchange, with in a limited time. Then old currency notes were seen thrown in garbage bags and were seen in the streets and at the beaches. People were harassed and there was hectic activity going on in the banks.

One day he announced a date for public hangings against the suspected anti-nationalists and the scene was horrifying. Public hangings were shown on TV and children were removed from the sight of such a chaotic event. For several years there prevailed the fear of repetition and people were frightened to be wrong listed. I was not accustomed to such changes and felt very much out of place. I prayed for relief and safety of locals. Foreigners were not involved. Leader formed 'People's committees' and they would form Assemblies to govern, but they were chosen few. And the system of governance was very much disorganized, but people had no option except to adjust with the routine.

Doctor told me that leader was involved in terrorist activities everywhere, as he was the board member of the group of his faculty, to evaluate the post traumatic stress subjected to the people who were forced to participate in such activities. There was beyond doubt his involvement in several countries for nothing, except satisfaction of his inflated ego. Everybody was working under stress and got along with their duties but with caution and reserve. Doctor was a far-sighted person and he could not see a long time of survival under such conditions. To add to our suffering, we had to face the discrimination for being expatriates. But people were plain and simple and God fearing.

They ascertained as though it was destined and lived on.

I had to live with my destiny. I became pregnant and the news was well received. I was taking extra care of my diet and put on regular checkups. There were few spotting of blood and I was provisionally diagnosed placenta previa, but without a confirmed diagnosis, because of the malfunctioning of ultra-sonography machine. I was advised complete bed rest for of the entire pregnancy course and we took additional care. Doctor's mother joined me to take care of the post-natal experiences. I was admitted to the hospital well in advance, a place which I hated most. I couldn't speak local language and it was a big barrier. Doctor had his duty obligations to fulfil but he continued visiting as often as he could. The ultrasonography machine, a new one was brought in and I was to scanned.

The duty nurse took me to the laboratory after climbing down the stairs and I started bleeding. The specialist carried me to the theatre and I was given anesthesia. When I woke up Doctor informed me about the infant in intensive care unit and that everything will be alright with time. I dozed off and couldn't remember the details thereafter. Later I was informed that our first born expired and Doctor had authorized the hospital to arrange for the burial. He was quite and thinking most of the time. His mother also was silent and prayed for us. Doctor booked our tickets to homeland and re-routed the travel through the pilgrimage center. We went to pilgrimage and prayed in unison for our forgiveness and relief. We did not exchange any word about the tragedy. No one is put to everlasting sadness, as sadness always follows relief. It was our faith.

It was alright for me to be sad. I could cry, sob and grieve. I could do it as anyone could do it. It is natural emotion of humans. So, I could be sad. But I didn't. I don't know why. Was I not prepared for any grief reaction? I thought of crying in isolation, as I was told it smoothens the pain. But I didn't have any pain. I thought of complaining to God. Complaining to others was purposeless. Everyone undergoes sadness. Was Doctor sad? He wouldn't share. He believed in keeping things to himself, more so if he feels sharing may not help. Crying and shedding tears are profound expressions of pain. But first pain has to be perceived to let you compensate for the relief it warrants.

Truth is revealed in the Holy book about the fact of life. Eventualities of realities of life. Every person's mind is unique to one. It cannot be compared with others. Only God gives the strength and courage to face the tragedies of life. Life in incomplete without sorrow. Only God can understand the philosophy behind this truth. All these thoughts were going through my mind. Am I pushing myself too hard? Did I miss out on anything, not to be neglected? It appears incomprehensible at times. There can be good times and bad times. I committed to myself not to discuss these issues with Doctor. I should meet up to my commitments. There is no way out.

We did what was possible. That's it. We gave our best, but it did not work out and probably it was not meant for it. We make the deals with all strings attached. We make mergers. We think it is right. What if it turns out wrong? The mergers cannot be called off. The conditions will get twisted and what will follow is tussle, a tug-of-war, a game. It was not my type I had been yielding to influences since very beginning and I had always been reluctant to negotiations. But I should not yield to injustice. But no injustice was done. It appears so, but who knows the God's plan.

The reason I think is several key elements are charged within us for their perfectness, their glad tidings, their aims and their goals. We could aspire for what we wish, but the bottom line is, we have to revise our formed opinions about our goals. They may be suitable or not. First opinions should not be formed quickly and if formed has to be revised. There will be compelling reasons for us to revise. There will be motivational dead zones in between. We can cross them un-hurt or absorb them hurt. The choices are difficult. The write off had to be settled within ourselves. The packages in front of us are always benefitting in the end. That is our faith.

We went home and life was back to normal. Time passed and the emergency vacation time was over and we returned back. Doctor joined his duty and I attended to the routine house chores. I got inflicted with urinary tract infection and was under treatment, with no relief. Doctor said it is a common condition among ladies for their short urinary tract and the source is most probably the toilets in malls and restaurants. A visiting professor in Urology came to the city and I was shown to him. He advised a series of X-rays after a contrast reagent was given and several shots of X-rays were taken, to visualize the cause. The reports came out normal and I was relieved. But curiously I forgot that I had already missed my period and was few week's pregnant when the intravenous pyelography was subjected. Doctor was alarmed but he kept things to himself. I could hardly understand the implications.

Meetings among Doctors were held to discuss my case. A group was in favor of medical termination of pregnancy for the fear of consequences. Doctor did not discuss anything about it with me. I was not even aware of the risks involved, but I knew that it was going to be a precious child. Especially after the fate of the first pregnancy. Doctor decided on his own to let it go. I was happy about the progress but hated to be carried to the same hospital for the follow ups. I had no idea what went wrong. I had no idea I had been conceiving my precious child when I was subjected to IVP. I had no idea what would be, the medical repercussions. I was feeling proud to become a mother soon, rather so soon. There are certain things which can't be helped. God had His own plans for us. We were contended with it.

MINDFUL ATTENTION

All very unpleasant dodging questionable civilities were Doctor's moves and all God forsaken subtleties were my countermoves. The victim was unfortunately an impetuous person like me, who was obliged to cater to garbage of humility, challenging the shadows of deepest fears of future. Separately, warily and in varying phases of confusion, I was targeted by whims and fancies of my so-called husband, who even otherwise could not be of any avail. The effect of his half lies or half-truths, as one puts it, should not have been given any attention by me anymore. He had an intuitive desire not to listen to these counterfeit contents but I could not resist the urge to highlight time and again, sagging his courage and decreasing his self-confidence.

What is wisdom? I don't know. No, I don't want to talk to the unwise. People who do not gray their hair in the sun are wise. But they may be greater fools under the sky. Is it a statement or an understatement? Wisdom for wise is tolerance to stupidity. Some wise mem and women thing it is related to genetics and some think it is acquired. What is it? It is the basic IQ levels or experience. Is it being learned or being a student learning still? It is not easy to recognize and not easy to forget. Wisdom is wisdom and we cannot go further to explain. Even wisdom like faith, belief, theology, philosophy is interpreted differently by different people. People are people. They will form their opinions and there are certain things which cannot be changed.

The old-time Barter's deals were wise, where both parties undertaking sales and purchases were contended with their deals. Today's online business is unwise, as the online competition puts the sellers to a turmoil. The seller has to collect the money first, shipping charges included and make the buyer to wait impatiently until the delivery takes place, while seller is waiting anxiously to face the charge backs, with additional fear of shipment getting lost or damaged in the process or after delivery and the buyer has to call the toll-free number which is actually charged, followed by sending emails for the intention of return and again wait impatiently to receive his shipment.

Wisdom is raising our children straight, to let them remain on a straight path, not to deviate into perverted ways, not to get crooked and not to go astray. Wisdom is training our children to become more dependable on themselves and to become efficient helpers in helping us to achieve our righteous goals. Wisdom is not sending children to medical schools, law schools, business schools and sports schools to get away with responsibility. They may strive hard but get nothing in return. Judiciary advocation, business ethics, medical knowledge and sports achievements are pre-mandatory to non-corrupt societies.

Wisdom is to make them wise in thought, feelings, conversation and faith. Through wisdom we can device increasing contentment, whether they are competing or detailing to convey and to interpret and also to introspect their own systems of congeniality to remain in peace and balance, both equally important. The difference is between inside and outside, the thoughts about inside and the thoughts about outside, as all religions are being taken casually. Old religious principles are becoming part of new pop culture and new pseudo-philosophy. The faith for a purpose in life is wisdom. This purpose has to be served by the creations of God.

Prophets of different faiths were tested for their wisdom, patience and sacrifice. Prophet Abraham was tested by God to sacrifice his progeny, the outside picture was that of an order to be executed, but the inside thoughts of the prophet were different. While performing this execution he was concerned about his fear of his followers reverting back to idolism. Now that wisdom is lost. Todays children are falling back to pre-historic times and involved in practicing the different kinds of idols, not the necessary statutes of gods, but era has changed them into other material satisfactions, which are their idols.

Idols of present days are the technological gadgets for fun, money, name, fame and position and everyone is after it, almost worshipping them. People are not interested in gathering and sharing wisdom, instead they are propagating and sharing their fake idols. The guidance from God is fabricated and each one is in search of their own goals, not the goals advocated by religious norms. In this procedure they are losing touch with reality and proper ideals to understand the purpose of our existence.

Why are we created, why are we sent to harmonize the social relations and what remains our purpose in life and afterlife. We cannot rely on Sunday schools for ultimate teaching required for the same. We need to ask ourselves the question that we cannot justify and remain defensive about not knowing. If we do not know we can always learn. We need to be good to the deserving, we need to help the needy. The learning, the education, the qualification, the experience and the wisdom is required to be responsible.

We need to come closer to one another, we need to socialize for our own good and the good of others. We have to train our minds to become more impactful in helping to achieve what we aspire. We have to be on the edge to help keep track of trusting one another. This has to be an important component of our project to come. We have to memorize first, rehearse then and start executing our projects. Memory of information is equally important, not because of its storage capacity but because of its capacity to be retrieved in times of need. We shouldn't forget the good or the bad. We shouldn't forget the considerations or the in-considerations. We have to keep a record of it to be able to use if time warrants, for the sake of learning from the past.

Past is past for brooding but past is present for learning and recouping and present is future towards the scope of progress we can make. Truth ultimately pop up from somewhere or nowhere, in unlikely circumstances, sometimes incomplete, sometimes misleading and sometimes half lies or half-truths. We have to make sound decisions from our experience, based on observation of the past, even if it has to be exhumed. The fondness of happy endings is an artifact but trustworthiness in people is a reality. Genes of wisdom can catch up with humans for their righteous paths to the destinations towards contentment. Wisdom is to learn to maximize both creativity and invention, without losing touch with reality, but wisdom cannot depend on memories, as memories are fallible.

Financial intelligence directs us to invest in assets, but assets are children not properties, bonds, business, etc. children are real assets and that was propagated by old times and Holy book. Children in another 10-15 years will be new community leaders and society representatives. It is not long time, rather it is just across the corner and the fruits will be provided to the world. I was thinking, deep introvert thinking. We ere returning home. The journey to our apartment was quiet and almost peaceful. It was a constant contrast to the bickering of the day before. My gaze outside the dark night was fastened dreamily on the lights and the nightlife of that place, putting it down to tiredness. Doctor also said very little beyond giving the street directions and the traffic signals. There was no scope of mischief left between us. I continued with my thoughts.

Patience is yet another criterion for the need to strengthen the society and the world. Patience is gratefulness for what is already provided by the almighty. There are problems around us and many trials waiting to be attended and in spite of all this if we show gratefulness to God, He will give the solutions with time. We have to show gratitude for His allowance of our existence and survival. Patience gives endurance, tolerance and forbearing. Learning to be patient is as good as getting acclimatized by hardships, which no one knows when they will crop up. Patience gives footing and stability and allow peace and balancing of ups and downs, which are a part and parcel of our coping resources. Intrinsic desires will blow out of proportion to harm us.

Wise people do not remember things wrongly, but it is other way, as unwise people do not even remember what to remember and what to forget. Out of all the stock of memories formed in their past. Today's memories are confabulated by technological advances and scientific developments making our minds skeptical rather agnostic against the older values. But old times were peaceful times and today's times are full of restlessness. Now we are occupied in hurried rituals only consuming time and getting us nowhere. The sciences of Anthropology, Psychology and Philosophy are carrying us into a chaos from where we are focused into convergence of lack of truth, half-truths or half-lies.

Religious teachings are being forgotten in this culture and the academics of modern thought is passing its legacy of non-existence of God, rather Atheism is creeping its claws into our traditions. Earlier God was considered supreme and belief in life after life was recognized. The very fact that the consequences of wrong doings will be questioned in after life, itself used to restrict the wrong doings. The predominant concept today is immediate returns in mechanisms, systems and material sciences. The focus is on this life, this time and this moment.

No doubt the infrastructures are being seen as the byproducts of these developments and are mesmerizing. Spirituality is replaced by mis-concepts of psychology and importance is being given to the body and not the soul. While the pre-modern society was governed by values of super-natural entities thereby seeing the signs to understand the existence of God and the purpose of creation of this universe. What was declared wrong is now acceptable and this transformation had led to the remarkable changes, like Marihuana is now a useful drug and legalized, homosexuality is now being considered a right and no more a disease. But this culture cannot sustain itself for long.

The wrong cults are now being registered as acceptable norms and this downfall in deviations will increase to magnanimous denominations and this distorted misguidance will lead to lack of satisfaction and lead to a search for happiness and contentment which will become non-existent. The net result will be imbalance in social values and demarcation of classes and the options left, would be to return to pre-modern times and to restore peace. This is the time we have to rise up to the occasion to face the reality, instead of turning our backs and pretending to be progressive. Two parables were given in the Holy book for explanation. Light is guidance and darkness is misguidance. This is spiritual analogy of our faith.

The tests will prove their results on the day of resurrection. The light will be sincerity of faith leading to good deeds, which will be rewarded. The amount of the glow will show the concept of bloom in the wisdom. The darkness will surround the deviants and desperate wrong doers. They will be in search of mirage which would fade away when approached and the destinations will get lost. The layers of darkness will be course and gross. The tides of the ocean will engulf the evil and guidance will not be made available. No one can influence other's conditions. From outside everything seems good but the inside will be ugly. From outside one can feel proud but the pride is a devil's workshop.

The feeling that they are better placed is condescending its own good. They are actually deprived of happiness and In constant pursuit to be happier. They try to get addicted to people, places, goods and ideologies, which does not satisfy them and the spark of light shown by the God is to introspect the right and wrong. We are supposed to correct our mistakes, errors and sins. These efforts will reward us with contentment in the end. It is better to be wise. Wisdom is submission to God. Wisdom is keeping peace, collecting pieces of peace and migrating. Wisdom is tolerance to stupidity, wisdom is search for critical remedies, wisdom is to antagonize abuse for use, wisdom is ignoring morbid letters and selecting black among whites.

Wisdom is raising voices to protect cruelty, wisdom is insight into our own weaknesses to gather strengths of personality predispositions. Wisdom is worship to one God, wisdom is praying with regularity to acquire discipline, wisdom is to find devotion to meditation to know the righteous path of life. Wisdom is to fast for testing our tolerance thresholds, wisdom is giving charity to balance the economics and wisdom is to be considerate towards others while offering pilgrimage. Wisdom is kind words spoken to the deserving. Wisdom is to remain between docile and aggressive and to stick to assertive behavior.

What else wisdom could be? Wisdom could be invocation for modesty, simplicity, humbleness and humility. Wisdom is analyzing our own anxieties, phobias, stresses and melancholia and obsessions and overcoming by wisdom and wisdom alone. Wisdom is allopathic medicine, thoroughly researched, wisdom is good clinical practice where drugs are marketed after the discovery of a molecule useful for an ailment and undertaking millions of dollars and decades of drug evaluation by phases of trials to know about their efficacy verses toxicity, early onset and delayed onset untoward effects. Wisdom can't be unresearched practices or usage of some empirical medicines after years and years of usage with some unclear results.

Wisdom is not organization of mind to undertake tasks and failing, wisdom is disorganized random work to get benefitted at the earliest, wisdom is essence of time and not wastage of it. Wisdom is not wondering but wandering for appropriate words to depict the emotions involved. Wisdom is faith and submission to it, wisdom is God sent Holy book and its preaching. Wisdom is fasting and not starving, wisdom is visiting Holy shrine all at one time and completing rituals keeping considerations towards others gathered for the same purpose. Wisdom is speaking softly, giving smiles, feeding the hungry and sharing the money with others. Wisdom is undertaking stretching exercises and meditating with thankfulness to God for His un accountable mercy and kindness.

Urdu poetry is wisdom and not obscenities of Bharath Nat-yam dance, sculpting four faces of past presidents is wisdom and not carvings of Ellora and Ajanta caves. Still art painting is wisdom and not venturing accidental capturing of pictures by a camera. Writing non-fiction is wisdom and writing fiction is not. Merging of identities is wisdom and not differentiating identities is not. Eating for hunger is wise and not for satiety to eat. Rain is a necessity and asking for right kind of rain is wisdom and not any kind of rain, which can even bring floods and hazards. A farm planter who is contended is wise and not the one gets harvest but craves for more.

A mother who gives an un-opened toy to her child to keep the enigma of surprise as long as possible is wise, as no sooner the toy is opened and exposed the child would play for sometime and would lose interest, asking for a new toy. House warming parties is a tradition which is acceptable but if the host is carrying the invitees to show the rooming capacities and amenities and utilities is unwise, as the similar tours given to them can be very disappointing. Wisdom is to judge certain facts revealed 1400 years before.

SUPERFICIAL WANDER

Doctor couldn't help except watching the events with lack of amusement and disgust. But at least he was conscious of stands taken by our sides and empty promises of possible drama not convincing. His claims of probable outcomes were becoming gloomy, my desires getting diffused into trivialities. My sanity was questioned on concentrations on little things and my control over the drama amazingly merciful. It was particularly overwhelming of me to react over such overcrowding of falsifications and I was aware of their existence forced by equal impacts earlier. The attached pains were felt, sufferings perceived and only then verification demanded. As a result, furies were channeled outrageously, words uttered hopelessly and exactions severing the relationships.

Doctor proved to have become different person. He would be kind at times, assertive at times and imperative at other times. He was a different person before and now is a different person altogether. Time changes people, time changes appearances, looks, figure, contours, features, wrinkles and tremors. The process of change with time and conditions. But I wanted his serious wit, ever serious humor and those tender embraces so special of him, that one feels like absorbing in them, which Doctor possessed I wanted to remain, with out any change. He was no doubt a different person from very beginning, he would show annoyance by stares, control by raising his pitch of voice and care by holding the hands. He does not believe in handling children until they are little grown, he would never impose punishments which appear like punishments, his worst reaction is withdrawal of love, which was a big punishment for who so ever want his care.

I was subjected to initial cultural, climatic and social shocks but I adjusted well with all these shocks so easily with Doctor's help. He was always available when needed. But I was wandering about his change, wondering for the reasons. But he believed in sharing things with people who could help, not who could not. He never shared his secrets with me, must be on purpose, maybe he was getting involved in affair with someone else. More open with less inhibitions, more cooperative and more vigorous than I am. I was abused in that sense too. Doing all the petty maneuvers by myself for him and not getting appraisal was abuse. Is he a case of Bi-polar illness, sometimes high and sometimes low? But that can't be true. These may be his mood swings, as people call it. But even his mood swings had a purpose, so they were not even mood swings. Then what were they?

He was a liberal man. Liberal to himself and liberal to me as well. He was guilty of something, which would not get portrayed or displayed. He would confide in me of his shortcomings and his long comings. That is not cheating. That is not loyalty also. Then what is it? I don't know and I don't want to know. We were happy as we were and I liked him, rather loved him and he never expressed any thing except an unseen care and concern for my needs, my desires and my wishes, timely or untimely. I had good time with him. His companionship transformed me from a village girl to a woman of substance, which of course I couldn't have done on my own. He would carry me everywhere, introduce me to his friends, ladies or gents, gentle or vulgar, bisexual or homosexual. To him it is their business to deal with it, not ours.

Or am I a sociopathic personality? Or those who consider me as one? People have not understood my straight forward nature. My well-wishing type. They try to demoralize, demean, and also depreciate me. They do not know my tolerance thresholds. When I cross them I can become one they wish? One woman misunderstood me and thought I have ridiculed her for not having conceived any children. I casually said 'I can do it for her' without meaning it but she was annoyed and made a big fuss. I advised her to see a specialist or even Doctor could have helped her. It was all well wishing and well meaning. I know Doctor has counselled many couples and helped them to consume their barren marriages. But there are retarded people who cannot understand intelligent suggestions. I can't help them. Nobody can, except God. But God also do not help those who do not help themselves. One un-lady like person also misunderstood my remark in lieu of my straight forward help and she mistook it as malicious intention. But it was her funeral not mine. So, I need not worry. I am not responsible for their below average IQ levels or lack of understanding of the norms. I intended good which was taken differently. Let them go to hell.

I was misunderstood by yet another woman who survived a natural calamity and blamed me for not asking her welfare, when her voice mail was full and did not accept any more messages. People should get the treatment they receive or deserved.

Doctor always used to repeat this phrase. I don't know what he meant. Neither I care. What I care was the Doctor's change of attitude, behavior and overall personality change. I should explore the reasons but he does not allow any probing. He is an open and shut case of a police file closed for ever. He started draining his pent-up frustration and was speaking less and less. But he wanted me to get acquainted with the women's hospital where I had to be admitted for my second caesarian section. The medical rule was first should be followed by the second, and third and fourth.

I had to start from the very beginning, from discomfort, to pain, to suffering and to go on and it looks like a lot of work with no breaks for any meaningful dialogue or carelessness. I also had lots of pursuits from happiness, to coolness, to prestige, to fame, to richness, to desires, to excel for an impact which was my ideal. Happiness never satisfied me, it did not allow me to sit back and relax, I could take eternal rest and allow time to lapse. I want to live a legacy as directed by God to share the truth, and it is to wait for judicious sanctions with results. I wanted to do something which can be remembered for long. Even I have to have selfish motivations to bring the desired change in Doctor and I was willing to sacrifice.

Doctor notified his administration to refer all calls from women's maternity hospital to him. It seemed a unique request and he was asked to explain the reasons and he did. He made them to understand that he wanted to expose me to the premises as often as possible to let me overcome my fear of that hospital which was developed and sustained. He started carrying me to that hospital, some times he would leave at the gate with watchmen, old and kind people who would serve me coffee or tea with watermelon or boiled eggs or whatever was available and some times he would carry me inside and let me get exposed to the corridors, wards and theatres and nurses and night shift duty Doctors. But I was still afraid of it.

There was unknown distancing and unseen indifference which was becoming evident for me, as I never had such difficulty in conversation with him as before, which I was facing now. His company which I used to long for at any cost, was not completely made available for me as before, with such openness and satisfaction, which I had been cherishing since long. It looked as if he has stolen my tranquility and patience, which he himself loved to retain and enjoy earlier, but something was missing in our relationship. My heart became restless and my mind wandered in all directions to find solace which I felt I deserved in his company. I wonder had his eyes had done some sort of magic on me that my inclination amounting to adoration was never felt before in me. I wanted him back as he used to be and as I desired him to be.

Firstly, I must concentrate on completing and publishing my book to get some recognition outside and then I could impress Doctor later. Rejection letters from publishers is indication to let me stop trying to become an author, I should look for some other occupation. Editor who has rejected my manuscript would do the same again. I was told by Doctor that I must be open for new chances and I must know the system to beat it. I had an option of going to self-publishing companies. They are cropping up every where and they don't even do the editing. I can get away with whatever I wish to publish.

I am sounding like a fortune teller, who may please me by saying that my book would sell very well. How it can be possible without the marketing support. With out paying a handsome money share to include it in New York times or some website with a lot of fan following. I am mistaken this time too. I have always been committing mistakes. My mistakes could be good for others but not for me. Doctor also tells me that I have to take risks to gain. I think I should leave things as they are with regards to book publication. Writing a book is not easy, it is task and a lot of mental imagery and comprehension difficulties and to bring the elements of surprise, which is most difficult.

It is also about time that I learn, follow, show etiquettes taught to me by Doctor. School never taught me any etiquettes, parents did not do so either. It was Doctor who took care of me in these aspects. School was a menace of memoirs. Memories of pain and suffering only. Memories of differentiation, distinctions, demarcations and demeanor. I also kept teachers uncomfortable. Male teachers only, as female teachers got along nice with me. It may be my precocious body or ignorant mind. I never minded male teachers squeezing my cheeks, or patting on my back, pinching my bottom or holding me from back. Female teachers used to be looking at me with either amazement or amusement. I was a favorite of my lady headmistress and she would give me chocolates, candies, assorted biscuits and what not, but I don't know why?

I don't even want to remember those times, or to keep them in my memories, or to write and document them, all those silly mishaps, funny adventures, intimate friendships, shyly correlations and everything, I want to erase all from my memory. I just want to remember Doctor's past, present and future. I might have been a cute little baby, grown into a traditional beauty and now embodied with a stranger whom I rely, depend and concert with. If I became attractive and appealing it was not my fault. If I developed a crush invitation from the other gender, it was not my fault. What is wrong with me if I am capable of becoming a center of attention for the men folk. But they are chauvinistic race. They have limited interests and limited short-term stands.

I remalned my original self. I had my own style and I tried mixing with other styles to make them comfortable. That probably was my mistake. People took advantage of my Innocence and mt appeal. I just wanted to put some equations right, even if have to divide or multiply. I like equations, as some are good. Some people light candles on their loved ones' anniversaries, some people cook cuisines which their loved one used to like, living or dead. They do that to bring some solace, some happiness and some joy. I don't do any of these things. I kept myself as original as I was.

But Doctor's change was adversely affecting me. It was becoming gloomy at times. Malice at other times. Some of his actions are wonderful and some are wonder less. Somethings kept wandering in my sphere and some became static. Some were turbulent some were stagnant. Some of my tactics worked, some didn't. some of my actions impressed him and some left no impressions. Some of my acts healed and some wounded further. Some things entertained him some bored him. I was at loss to understand what is the way out? I was afraid if I try anything new it may turn out to be disastrous, devastating and distressing to him. He was already in stress. He was reluctant to confide in me. It may not have been worthy.

He was not a fake person, he was righteous most of the times. He would be blank if he prefers to be and he would be colorfully cheerful if he want it to be. Some of his responses were stupid but some were intelligent. His attitude was cherishing, real and delightful but sometime it was adopted, freaking and scary. I was honest with him, I confided my mistakes, some purposefully done some mistakenly done. But I loved attention, I liked admiration, I adored appraisal. I will have to change. But for what? I cannot mend or bend anything. I would crack at the slightest bit of additional pressure. I would grope for a straw to support. I was invited to change which I failed to adopt. I ventured into new land without any means, measures or resources. I was hurting myself.

I had always listened to my heart and it had always led me to the truth. I had considerations for others and more so towards Doctor. Considerations which distinguish animals from human beings. I was asking for favors, in spite of knowing that favors cannot be asked lightly to be rejected lightly. I will also learn sooner or later. Doctor always used to say, 'A man keeps learning all his life'. I wanted to be the rightful heir of my throne. What an irony of facts, some comical some tragical. Some racists are picking up 'Yezids', a small clan of old times, who massacred innocent people of those times, now reduced to counts on fingers and these red necks are bringing refugees for asylum, while parents of US born citizen children are getting deported. Is this a system or parody of system? They will regret later.

The saddest news was that the biggest terrorist activities done by Israel and my homeland country, around their neighborhood are now pledging in coalition to fight against terrorists. The irony of politicians that all the celebrated movie stars, cricketers and business tycoons are contesting in elections in their own countries and winning to become corrupt leaders to wage formal wars against corruption. Democrats are talking and republicans are talking, both against each other and talking never seems to end, as though they are women folk who according to one study spend an average of 5 hours per day in gossip talking against one another. I was getting tired of such news. News anchors should be removed and newsrooms should be closed and locked. What a pity there was news that women folk are watching more porn films to explore their sexuality, are actually being highlighted by those promiscuous types who are trying to justify and those are the ones who are deprived of bisexual surrogate partners.

HONEST DISHONESTY

Allowing ourselves to suffer to the extent and floating ourselves into the possibilities of not being able to face with the ground realities, which allowed us to escape our liabilities. It became a circuitous fear mongering to gain some understanding, some sympathies by none. A blinding chaos was created by these miscreants, they intended response and we protested with the blurred presentation. I disapproved of Doctor's humility and my perceptions were numbed buffered by hordes of sense and a platform was created to sense the victimization. I was crushed but the good thing is he remained intact, but appeared to be losing the balance of reasoning, peeping into jammed recesses of hopes, half destroyed by the way things were put.

I was getting nervous at times, no most of the times, but I never used to get nervous before. Now that I am nervous, my nervousness in this case may get repetitive. Instead of anxiety, generalized or focused, I should better displace it to any object, situation or subject to become phobic. Better still is I associate my nervousness to any body part and throw a fit of hysterical aphonia, aphasia, blindness or paraplegia or something. It would be better if I dissociate it to myself with my memory to become a case of hysterical amnesia or even coma. I think I am nervous because I am not able to please Doctor, I am not able to earn any living, and there comes the role of charity. Charity in my faith is given a lot of priority. Giving a date palm is a charity, smiling to others is a charity, kindly spoken words to an abused is a charity and donating in millions by somebody deceased to make it a charitable hospital is also a charity.

All the goodness I did or dealt with was not charity, all the variables I did to please people is not charity. I should do some charity to Doctor, even if he deserves or not. All the good deeds which I did were distortions of reality. All the other things are part of the show. I must get clean to become a character of my show. I should not play around, otherwise my existence will get jeopardized. Existence is necessary for recognition, recognition is necessary for impact, impact is necessary for popularity, popularity will come with excellence, a profanatory condition for contentment. Forget it. I will not be able to make it. I am just a person who is fantasizing, who is hallucinating what I desire, not the visual hallucinations of a grieved person nor auditory hallucinations of a split personality. It is different.

I have to be optimistic. Optimism is a show off of pessimism in a reality situation. Life is cheap, idols of gods are cheap. Anybody can buy it. It is a deviational choice and it is a devastating tragedy. So cheap that anyone can buy, like a soft cool drink in summer and hot coffee in winter. That's all. It only concerns four seasons. I could have done with three but four is fine. No problems with seasons. Actually speaking, it is 6 months of grey, 2 months of white, 2 months of green and 2 months of multi-color. They are themselves a liability, In east or west. What a life to live in shades of grey and very little color. If this is reality, so be it. Not much could be done there. Just an expression as one can bring in externally without any passion for the same. Meaning acting out. No need to internalize emotions to digest, assimilate, circulate and energize it. They are emotions and not nutrients.

God, let's insert some music with sunrise and sunset, melodies of rhymes and rhythm. I can include interludes later. But for now, music is important. Music could be hot, music could be pop, music could be orchestrated screaming in group or singly, as music is necessary. Music is harmonious melody, music is dis-harmonious shouting, music is recreational, music is revival and music is life to be resurrected and to be resonated. It is my business and nobody's else. I should mind my business and others should mind theirs. Each one has one's own responsibility. Authors should write whether publishers put subject matter or not. Writers have to write with their flow of thoughts.

Thoughts coming gradually or flooding without control. I must desensitize myself, and there are two ways I can handle it. Either by gradual exposure or by onslaught of overwhelming ideas. Whatever I like and whatever time it suits me. I have to please Doctor, I have to trust my instincts, instincts have never helped me. Basic instincts, inspired by introspection, inspired by insight, inspired by enlightenment and inspired by creativity. Graduate in psychology, masters in philosophy and Doctorate in mythology. Life is good and death is not bad, police is good but thief is not bad, homeless is good but shelter is not bad. Journeying by flight is good but by train is not bad.

I think God decides the choices for us to choose from. It is not His mistake it is ours. We are unsure of what is right and wrong. That includes me. I can't choose the right choice, neither I can be re-incarnated or re-born. I can't be Lincoln, Kennedy, Obama or even Washington. I had to be what fate chooses me to be. I can't include some complimentary choices in them, I can't have petty likes or dislikes about the choices. I can cook for Doctor, to his taste, I can do his laundry, I can submit myself to his needs, I can chat on social media, I can read books, I can paint or do embroidery. I have no control over my spiritual formation, spiritual wisdom, spiritual faith, and spiritual destiny to choose companions, children, in-laws, relatives and friends or even acquaintances.

The fact is if seed is planted, a concept has to take place. It will take place if it is destined to, but there are exceptions to the rule or rather exemptions, seeds themselves can be malformed, premature, strong or disordered. I have learnt what is taught to me. I have not deviated from teachings or preaching. I have not fabricated or invented or discovered new teachings. The learnt teaching was total and final. I have no doubt made some mistakes, some fiction, some non-fiction, some documented and some undocumented. Now the question is how I can make choices of importance, not the petty ones. Relevant, coherent, virtual or real choices. Lot of good things happen for the good of it. It is known and does not need any elaboration or explanation or clarification. I know Doctor does not believe in complaints and explanations. I am going to stick to that.

I am not doing any arson, burglary or theft to become an accessory to crime. I hate prisons and I also hate hell. I am a straight person with straight mind set. I am clear person who does good business with myself. It is none of my business or anyone else business to get involved in other people's businesses. I am not a bad person to begin with or to end with. I only have to make a better effort to be good. Just mere trials will not do any good. God sees efforts and people see results. I remember this phrase too well to forget, in spite of being forgetful. I am a clean slate of not a first grader but of 7th grader, who can wipe it really clean and don't leave any chalk marks.

I have not done any wrong to be forgiven for free. I have not broken any laws of the land, I did not get any speed tickets or parking tickets, as I don't drive rashly, which I used to do earlier. I have not seen Indo-Pak war, or Iran-Iraq war or US-Vietnam war, which were big mistakes realized later. How much wrong one can do by making mistakes as no one else, I am going to pay for my mistakes. I have to pay for myself. By paying for them, I am getting accrued compounded interest, which seems higher than the principal. That is enough learning in a life time. I have grown up and I am now a different person. I am different not differed, one must know the difference. I have transformed from old stone age menial worker to a scholar who could write books and publish them.

I cannot be boisterous. Boasting, bragging, jealousy and pride are like wood worms. They eat a person from inside, make the person hollow. Powdered to powder. I have to experience this truth. Truth as it sounds and experience as it is perceived. Not tingling and numbness of extremities denoting deficiencies. No, that is not all. Experience is like vibrations bringing back harmony. Experience of sensations arousing natural instincts, to protect or harm in self-defense. That is an experience I have yet to learn. I have just been taught hard earned experience to be wise but remaining a fool. I still can't help many things. I can't help my pressure of thought, thoughts racing, thoughts getting blocked or interrupted. I can't solve quizzes or puzzles. I am fond of kids, but kids do like me as well.

I know God wants us to be patient and to meditate, directly in conversation with Him. God alone can help. He can provide sources to provide help, which we may not know. From friends, strangers, lottery and unseen treasure. No one else can, except God. I don't know like my pet cats, which I don't have then. I love God, I love Doctor, I love my friends and children to be, I love my friends and some

Doctor's friends. I can't help it. I want to see myself in a different light, from a different angle, and then I have to persuade myself of my beliefs then I can convince Doctor and lastly the system which prevails anywhere. I want to make poor, richer and rich poorer. I will do it someday, if not now.

I know I am influenced easily by anyone. That is because I believe in people. I am also influenced by these electronic gadgets, which are emerging one after the other. I need to detoxify myself with magnetic reasoning, something magical to flush out all from my system. Clear like a primary school student's slate. If my body gets clean my mind will also get clean. Clean like glass, mirror, bedsheets which Doctor wants, as he removes invisible specks from them and clean like cutlery and dishes. I will make everything clean, including stars, sky, moon and if possible sun spots. I can get involved, but what about dirty linen, dirty trucks, dirty people, dirty tricks they play.

I can't get profound spiritual wisdom all of a sudden. I need time and I have to earn it by hard work. Self help first and then help others and then become social worker to help the society. But firstly, I have to believe in myself, believe in Doctor, which is not easy at times. I will have to do something, that is my purpose, that is why I have migrated. I have left my home, my parents, my friends, my brothers I cannot include, as they are parasites. But I left my accessories, my culture, wedding invitations, peeps from our window and climate, culture, people and city.

My life seems to be empty, pointless, immature, vacant and disorganized. I don't like systematic lives, as machines work systematically and I work randomly. I am a human being with ups and downs, highs and lows, vacancies and placements, deprivations and fulfillments, punishments and achievements. There has to be a balance in everything, faith teaches us to keep balance, and to maintain it in spite of conflict of interests, conflicts of civil rights, then I can do whatever I like, whatever I choose, whatever I wish, whatever I feel and the I can write whatever I want. I don't want to regret later, firstly, it will be too late and secondly it is foolish to do and to regret later. It is against wisdom. And I have to be wise.

I have become a pain in the neck, may be because I jumped from one continent to another, one language to another, one world to another, one community to another. I can take care of the pain in my neck but I can't take care of others being a pain in my neck. I am not responsible for the division of our sub-continent, I am not responsible for Iqbal's dual nation philosophy, or Gandhi's non-violence, or Kennedy's assassination. I can't feel guilty of other sects, the divisions of faith, world wars, or so-called UNO peace negotiations, or board's decisions for the Nobel prizes.

I am just a co-worker of God, a slave to follow His Holy book's directives. Not like a co-payer of covered insurances, or a co-author of a book unknown to me, or a co-partner of a company going in losses. I am being a part of volcanoes erupting, tornados wiping cities, floods evacuating inhabitants, politics dividing states, storms engulfing masses or earth quakes smashing sky scrapers. I am only a part of life of Doctor. He should be questioned for my wrong doings or even these pseudo-philosophical talks. I get fed up with all this at times. More so with Doctor. He is showing such pretentious behavior, manipulative behavior, unwanted behavior and abusive behavior. He was somebody earlier and he is someone now. He is s game player, poker player and winning player.

Now after all this Doctor is asking me to be a glory into his life. I can't be that great. I can't do anything to please him. He has no time for my silly thoughts, mindless interpretations of his attitude and he has no time to even listen to my grievance. He is occupied by his doctrines, theoretical, hypothetical, true or false. I don't know. What I know is he is abusing me. I was getting concerned about him and even in spite of showing considerate manners, he is not pitiful to myself. I think I am seeking attention from him or I am getting deluded by morbid jealousy. I think I should submit myself to Euthanasia or I should become a complete amnesic of the past.

I am beginning to hate his liking for gun-violence as much as his terrorist tendencies. I am beginning to hate his guts as much as home country's PM's guts. I should not choose to believe that truth is different. I should make believe that truth is truth. I should not yield to his injustice. I shouldn't become a victim of domestic violence. Doctor himself told me in so many words and then he denied. I have to take it seriously and fight for it. Fight until it is eradicated and I should stop all of it and stop for good. Abuse is not segregated by caste or creed or education or ignorance. It is an animal instinct which happens everywhere. I don't believe in the dictum of Doctor that if 'rape become inevitable, the just lie down and enjoy it'. It cannot be enjoyed by women rather it maybe by men folk. This is a biological difference, between capital 'P' and non-capital 'p'. It has some psychological concept with variables.

UNFAITHFULLY FAITHFUL

Doctor's formed opinions are actually biases. Having taken 'abuse' for so long, I had to stop it as normal insanity, as function at a level below normalcy. These decrees are damn near impossible to take any more, not progressive of a forming relationship which actually is abnormal sanity and nothing else. There were some unwanted mishaps blown out of proportion and I was succumbing to it, to the extent of getting inflicted by apprehensions and miserably coping up with the resent which is no worth.

Doctor was a wise man. His behavior must have some justifications. He had specific definitions of wisdom. He said even God does not approve of stupidity. He had one hundred percent tolerance to stupidity. That itself makes him wise. In his books, 'Miranda Declaration' is unwise. As it completes a formality, statement uttered in haste like a child memorizes a poem, to notify the culprits or suspects not to confess their wrong doings to face the verdict accordingly. Instead they are coaxed to remain silent, as things spoken could be used against them, until their corrupt attorneys arrive and advises them alternatively. Then what follows is 30% of innocents land up in prison and the balance enjoy their life casually.

On the contrary Mafia's 'Omerta Oath' is wise, as they believe to remain silent to keep up to their word and keep secrets to themselves about their families and friends and may become martyrs in dignity and honor. In Doctor's opinion there is not much difference in Capital 'Ps' and Capital 'As', as both sell their potential, one for their bodies and the other for their mind. Both have short survival span. One can live as long as one remains young and one after a particular age as long as they can sustain. Both has to keep transient relations with clients or publishers. Firstly, when their skins are stretched and secondly when their skins are wrinkled. Those who play around with words like Doctor are wise people and those who try to coin new words like scholars are not wise. Those who get something out of nothing are wise and those who get nothing out of everything are not.

I have zero knowledge and zero experience of people and cannot check and control bad guys. I have full knowledge and full experience to control good guys. I have zero distractions meaning, I can get distracted easily when deregulated. We have to be smart in driving seats and not sweating out in the back seat. I should have a theory or a hypothesis if not proof. I have to do something. Doctor says, wisdom differ from time to time, from region to region, from custom to custom. Wisdom for some is stupidity for others, pride is not wisdom, humility is wisdom. I may be wise or unwise, fair or unfair, clear or unclear, whatever it has nothing to do with wisdom. Wisdom has a different meaning in history, different meaning in faith and different meaning in literature. Why should I worry.

I should be straight. Talk about straight path, straight lines, parallel lines, not crossed lines or crooked lines. I must be right like right angle. Wisdom can be out grown, wisdom can be reaped, wisdom can be punched, wisdom can be borrowed or stolen. A wise toddler is better than an unwise adult. Anyone could be wise or unwise. Getting drawn is wise and drawing the drawn is not. Becoming famous is wise and infamous unwise. Being loved is wise and being hated is not. Getting in time is wise and getting late is not. Having few things is wise and having many is not. Dictating is wise and getting dictated is not. Stopping on signals is wise and jumping on crossings without cameras is also wise. Tenancy is wise and ownership not. Wisdom is tricky. It is an art, a craft and a tact. Financial intelligence is wisdom and spend thrifting is not. Training for money management is wise and getting trained is not. Believing in one God is wise and believing in many gods is not. Acceptance and contentment is wise and greed and intolerance is stupidity. Getting things done your way is wise and getting things done other's way is not.

There is not a man born still, who could claim to be wise. Well this is not an essay or a non-fiction or a fiction. It is admixture of all and admixtures are wise. Admixtures are different bindings of different compounds with different bonds which I will be from now on. I am moving, I am in motion and motion rolls weight and mass and I will grow. I will be ahead of time and these hardworking Doctors who study all life and remain unhappy and patients who get sick often, seek a prescription, get well and are happy. Designers are wise and buyers of designer's merchandise are not. What am I writing? I am not a writer, rather I am a reader. I am not a speaker, rather I am a listener. I am not an author, rather I am a publisher, earning well.

Wisdom is available everywhere. One has to pick it. Pickers are wise and losers are not. Success is not wise, as you may get fake grandiose ideas about yourself and cannot sustain it, rather failure is wise, as you can learn and re-learn and succeed in the long run. Emotions are stupidity and lack of emotions is also stupidity. Indifference is wisdom and lack of it is also wisdom. Some scientific theory suggested a hypothesis that major mental illnesses are emotional and not of intellect. But getting over stressed, or over cautious, or over anxious or over obsessive is not wise. One has a preformed premorbid personality with natural defense mechanisms. A neurotic will never cross the borders of psychosis.

God is wise, prophets were wise, believers were and are wise, atheists are unwise and hypocrites are unwise. They will have to revise their formed opinions in the end. Wisdom is impressing people and improvising people. Goals of wise people are their formed opinions and goals of stupid's like wise. People living for themselves are wise and people living for others are not. Affectation is wise and affect lessness not. Normalcy is wise, living abnormally is also wise, so don't be wise just fool around and be happy. This book would appear like a non-fiction about wisdom, but it is not. It is a fictitious fiction for the unwise, to just get entertained. It appeared so in the beginning that it is about wisdom, who lack it, but it turned out to be fun, frolics, amusement and recreation.

People I know who play video games or watch cartoons in their spare time consider themselves as wise, people who write screen plays and who make 'B' grade movies are wise, people who use words occasionally are wise and who use frequently are unwise, and people who talk in excess are not wise and who talk in laconic replies are wise. Simple phrases for communication are unwise, complicated long phrases are wise, simple plain phone users are unwise and smart phone users are wise. Tragedies are wise and comedies not, grief is unwise and relief is wise, happiness mongers are unwise because they lack it and want it and sorrow mongers are wise because they lack it and do not want it.

Great poetry is generated by sadness and ordinary poetry is written by fools. All these terms are relative, everything could be interpreted by double meanings and could be antagonistic to each other, there is no standard criteria of wisdom. Extremists are fools and balanced people are wise. I was unwise as I stick to Doctor's wisdom and sincerely followed it. My Doctor is wise as he married me and abused me in a different sense and lived a life of comfort, while I suffered in attempts to please him day and night, nights mostly as he was away for work in the day. My brothers were unwise as they never had any gainful employment and came to nobody's use. The were also unwise as they lived a life of disgrace and discomfort, always complaining.

There are always wise and fools around, some live casually and die unrecognized and some live shamefully blaming others and some live under a single roof and some live in open spaces, under the sky. My father was unwise as he loitered in the open yards of civil courts carrying files all his life and would have preferred to die in the court yard, if possible. My mother was equally unwise as she faced hardships in raising her children and got abused by them in her old age. Poor lady she selected her daughters-in-law and was maltreated by them, one blaming her for having done black magic on her family of fools, as only wise can contradict the existence of black magic and fools believe in it. This is all about the wisdom in a nutshell.

But more than anything else what bothered me more was the change of attitude in Doctor. Is he cheating on me? Has he found another soulmate which he is planning to impose on me? Is there any face prettier than mine which has attracted him? Is he in extra-marital relations with his lady colleagues or plenty of nurses working under him? Does some girls get attached to their opposite genders who are already married for transient temporary biological needs? I didn't know and I couldn't dare to encounter these subjects with him. He apparently cared me enough. He helped me in all other matters, where I needed help. He satisfied me in all respects. Then what was the secret? What was the case scenario in my absence which is distracting him so much? Time went by and I got into labor. I was carried to the same maternity women's hospital.

No sooner I was admitted I was anaesthetized and I went into deep slumber. I remained dazed and confused and my precious child was nursed in observation. She was brought to me with smiling faces of acquainted Doctors and nurses. All were praising her beauty. She was cute and pretty, but I didn't feel any attachment. Doctor took special permission or my discharge and signed for suture removal of my caesarean section at home. Doctor was happy and relieved, but I refused to carry the child home. The child was left on the cradle and Doctor took me to the car. Incidentally he found a friend living with bachelors in the parking lot and requested him to carry the child to his home to be collected later.

It was later I came to know the facts about the hazards of X-rays upon neonatal infants, the misery Doctor went through all those later months about the fate of delivery and all the details, which clarified my confusion about the secrets behind

Doctor's changed attitude. I even came to know how his bachelor friends were attempting to feed the crying baby with biscuits, chocolates and soft noodles, while she was in their custody. I slowly got adjusted to the routine but used to cry when baby used to cry and again Doctor shifted her to bottle feeding on a time schedule and not on demand.

For initial few days my breasts got engorged and were painful and Doctor used to apply some soothing cream to let me feel better. Those applications had other repercussions, which got satisfied by him. All went well except the aperture size of the pacifier nipple of the feeding bottles and a team of pediatricians were called, all Doctor's friends who were discussing the hole size and my friend, an experienced lady took the feeding bottle, heated a needle and punctured the nipple and the child was happily sucking the milk and sleeping well. All neighbors and friend's wives gathered and praised the beauty of my child. Doctor received telegrams of congratulations and everything went well. He took the charge of feeding his child and me as well. We both started gaining weight.

Life came back to normalcy and the outings, shopping and visiting was rescheduled and I started enjoying the routine. Meetings of the block's ladies were continued and small talks and small exchanges were all very pleasing and I still wanted some elderly lady's presence specially to bathe the baby, but somehow, I managed by keeping the baby on my bare legs and applying oil, messaging her before applying soap and bathing her, of course with the help of Doctor. Now I was unsure whether I was abused or he was being abused by me. I also wondered why my biological needs increased with time, which needed satisfaction immaterial of Doctor's exhaustion, after heavy day's work schedule with additional mental stress of medical board's duties.

I was glad that a neighbor spinster nurse from the same maternity hospital was regularly attending us, helping us in petty household chores. I saw her exaggerated interest in Doctor and exaggerated care for my needs. She used to brush pass hands, shoulders, bosom with low neck cut shirts with Doctor but nobody seemed to mind and I also did not mind these exchanges. She was voluptuous and gorgeous in body and friendly in manners and helpful to me in Doctor's absence. I myself used to wonder at her cleavages and body contours and had an eye of appreciation for her voluntary help. She insisted that she participate in the ritual of baby baths and I allowed her extended gestures of bathing both of us. I was not sure of her lesbian tendencies or appeal with curious smiles and glances towards the Doctor.

While I was resting I could occasionally over hear some whispers and bristles of clothing from the kitchen or living area and few giggles of other nurses who used to attend from neighborhood. I was happy still, as I knew Doctor is liberal in such matters and I had company indoors of my age girls exchanging small talk, jokes and laughs. Once I noticed another shade of lipstick on Doctor's shirt and without my asking he said the girls collide with me in routine movements indoors or outdoors. I was still happy as I had no problem of passing time and a baby to care for. And for that matter I got back the Doctor's original humor and interest in me. My parents were happy, Doctor's mothers were happy and we were happy. I was getting extra attention from everybody along with varied cuisines and additional gifts for me and my child. She was turning out into a coquettish baby and we took photos and posted them back home. I was grateful to God for all the favors given to me. More than anything Doctor's mood was stabilized and he was back to his original self.

That spinster nurse was also regularly visiting our house and because of shift duties at different timings. But she was a nurse and that too of a maternity hospital and it must be a regular routine work for her to be accustomed to female bodies. She suggested oil application to mothers is equally healthy as that for babies and she used to insist me to get undressed and started the same routine for both of us. She also mentioned saving extra work of drying my clothes and changing them more often than required. Curiously I started liking the massage and bath as much as my baby and as much as the nurse. I used to get relaxed and refreshed and used to sleep well. We remained friends and I must have been getting over valued ideas for nothing. Interestingly Doctor had no objection so there was no problem from any side.

ADVOCACY OF DOCTRINES

It frightens me to even think of sustenance of such trends and traits, which can be interpreted as victimizing yourself to avoid coming out of vicious cycle of abuse. Over years I have learned to discern the truth, truth spoken as believed, convinced of its weight-age and ominously substantial of its worth. As for me, there are still assignments to be done in concordance with norms, practicalities to be dealt with and common sense to be stretched out to contribute to common understandings of society. Certain secrecies got prolonged beyond limits, curricula of relationships incompletely formed and maintained, pending further evaluation.

I wanted my newly developed plans to explore the world, the demographic profiles of different cultures existing in different geographical areas, different histories buried in the different zones, I wanted to see the different vast lands of different continents with different climatic conditions. Never to get tired of roaming around. Never to change the contents of my thoughts, never to lose my memoirs which despised me earlier. I did not execute sentiments which were against my own objectives. I wanted to make my own goals of life. For the present I want to keep silent, suppress rigorous thoughts emerging subdued and killed. My thoughts appeared restless souls inviting me to other restless ventures. I wanted to be the primary source and supporter of my subversive designs, which I myself had fueled for my life to go on.

I realized my condition regarding the misguidance I received by scholars, whom I barely know. Their imitable principles of selfless love, I had for the humanity at large. I wanted recognition and respect from humanity for which I had plans, unknown still, unfinished and unspoken still. I wanted all to beseech me by their crooked imaginations and programs they have framed for me. I lacked the instilled religious guidance, required of me, to propagate the faith and belief in oneness of God, the almighty. I wanted to aspire for a literary fame of all sovereign, secular and impartial religious people. I wanted to live the ambitious agony of survivors like me. I was beginning to hate my own prudence, that petrifies and blinds me of all rights to the preservation of my own rights. I felt I had become a putrefied calamity in myself, miserable selfish soul with no considerations for others.

Let me be the pseudo-philosophical preserving the instruction of life here after, with my writings, doctrines and ideologies I have formulated for my own cause. The basic basis of cause and effect theory and the hypothesis of cost-benefit ratios. I want to receive the appraisal of liberals, not extremists and not conservatives. I have the obligation to open the eyes of the societies, to make them understand the contrast of object materialism plaguing the communities to be precise. My directives should end and the Holy book's directives should reach the hearts of all, they are meant for. I was getting tired of carved faces, encrypted titles, persistently closed glad tidings and consentingly open desires of people. I am getting afflicted by frailty of mind, impeaching my skills, my doubts and my liberties.

Now the loneliness has become clearer to me, the horizon's view which was a cult has now become dearer to me. I better start with eating the blank papers of my manuscript, burn the books intended to be published to give warmth to the homeless, beggars, liars, cheaters and vendors. I remember Doctor told me that he intended to write a book, which he would do some time, about the worst cases he has encountered in his career, whom he had managed to wellness and resumption to health.

He had never completed yet and may never do, as he had become indifferent towards his cases. He had a lot to handle and a lot to candle. I would tell him that I care for him, even if I didn't intend to. For the present I should have no worries, no apprehensions, no obsessions and no fears.

I wonder why always I am filled with Doctor's reflections, how much I loved him and how I would continue doing the same. Presently I was kept in restless silence and depthless calm, which soon would be threatening my existence. Only his voice echoes in my ears. When I hear the wind slapping at the window panes, reaching me through gazing hinges I feel closer to him and get warmth out of lingering love which I feel is sinking in the intensity of the feelings for me. As a sea of wave-less elaboration of impending storm. To note the evolution of habits of how he used to bear with me, the events of my notoriety which he used to ignore and my tantrums which he used to absorb in him. I was blessed by the shadows of his adorable appearances and my wontedness for him, bestowed by God's kindness. I still hope the clocks return, time returns to those merry joys of my life.

I was looking for the grasp of history, which it seems to me that those days will be returned to me untouched, unharmed and un-embarked. I looked back with glory and mystified fun at the old times, which were so joyful and so jubilant and world seem to endure my bearings to be given back to me again. How time passes by and within few years of my companionship incomprehensible to me and the happiness achieved in Doctor's company was still being recollected, as though happened a day or two days before. I want him to see my writings with dedication by poetic verses in his praise and worth. They will be my duty to bind myself within them and to be loved by generations to come. I felt distressed by the need to censor my passions for him.

It was understandable that Doctor was called to assist his home country's embassy and consulate work at our station, for which he was getting appraisal, but I failed to understand his involvement in covert terrorists group governed by the present governance and applauded by the leader of the country where we were expatriates. Somehow, he understood the leg pulling and the caution he had to play to remain a law-abiding citizen of his home country. Otherwise I used to wait and wait long hours for Doctor to return home, tired and exhausted and sleep immediately to continue with the routine for quite some time. The representative involved was a thin, lean and bearded man who had become a regular visitor at our place and I was beginning to hate him for becoming my rival.

It so happened that Doctor's friend reported the matter to the people's committee's office and the fabricated housing complexes were raided by armed police personal and the representative was hand-cuffed and carried in the night but brought back next day morning but it turned out to be the end of the drama to follow and life came back to normalcy. We were back to the same routine of evening strolls, with stroller to carry our daughter, we started visiting nearby hill stations, new beaches to be explored and Doctor carried me to all places with him. It looked as if his life is incomplete without me. Once we went to a distant beach in company of eastern European Doctor friends and their families. It was clear water and white sand. All changed into swimming suits and very few were wearing single piece suits. Most of the white ladies and girls of all ages were wearing two-piece suits of varying sizes and I was feeling shy.

Doctor pulled me into sea water with my clothes on and I tasted the salty water with distaste. My clothes fabric clung to my body and I found myself exposing my curves to all the playmates on the beach. The beige color turned out as my skin color and I felt very different. The males were looking at me with amazed eyes and some kind of hunger in them, as though they would eat me alive, if allowed. Curiously I liked the importance I was getting. We splashed water at each other and it was all a different of amusement to me. As the cargo ships were boarding their merchandise at the dockyards, we were getting our amenities through Doctor's contacts. We never ran shortage of anything.

Once he took me to Sudanese camp and the scene was very ugly with near naked men moving with ease making me un-easy. I looked the other way and all ways, were the same. They offered their specialty cuisines and Doctor joined them in a singe large plate and I remained hungry to eat the dinner at home. The scenario at the East Asian nurse's quarters was not much different than that of Sudanese camp with the difference that instead of males there were females in different stage of dressing up to overcome the shyness, typical of their origins. The group with Philippines spinster nurses was more vulgar than the rest. Doctor didn't make anyone feel that we are strangers and that was an art I didn't possess.

Doctor was back to normal and I was back to normal. We had good times together, which resulted in me getting pregnant again in a couple of years of time. We also made a visit to home country with sponsored tickets and paid leave and a lot of other privileges as airlines vouchers for domestic travel and went back home with gifts and tokens of gratitude from the government, which Doctor served. Back home everybody was happy to receive us and we went to neighboring state to pay homage to Doctor's father, who was buried there. We stayed in a good hotel and saw the infamous caves of 'Ajanta and Ellora'. I didn't like the sculptures but went along with the group, wondering the need of such excavations and the need for their display to public where families were visiting with children and seem to be appreciating the art behind the sculpting.

Doctor's father was considered an equal-Ent to saint and his gave was spread over with green cloth and flowers. We prayed for him and returned. There was no expression on Doctor's face, and I felt he was not much attached to him or rather he hardly knew him, as he was a toddler when his father demised. But he had pathological attachment to his mothers, both real and surrogate, who were getting older with time and were forcing Doctor to return back to spend time with them. After our return he described the hardships his mothers went through after becoming young widows and took care of their children with as much as they could afford with meagre pension and police medal allowance, renting the premises and duly sub-letting it with others to share the expense.

In a grave serious mood Doctor described how he spent his childhood giving private tuitions, selling his paintings, studying on scholarships and book funds. I believe after his mothers had to leave their husband, a lifestyle of affluency to contemplate their responsibility of raising children with limited grants, making their children to walk long distances for school and brought them up to become specialists. He felt compelling reasons to honor their request and discussed plans to return home for good. I didn't want to lose the lavish lifestyle I was accustomed to. I believe they were young widows and faced sacrifices of challenging tasks to while away their time. Doctor showed me black and white old photos of their glamorous lives and their youth and beauty.

The fleet of servants they were served with, the club activities of noble ladies of a big civil honor. They had a pair od Doberman dogs with a servant to look after them. They had wardrobes full of embellished garments to wear and specially made Victorian cuisines to relish with. He was unhappy with their decision of remaining single mothers and not re-marrying to find new-found loves and graces. Doctor's mind was always full of illustrations of their pretty faces and lovable gestures of concern for their kids. He kept elegant thoughts as their memoirs and was high with pride for his mothers and their bravery.

The well spent time of their youth followed by a continues struggle which they faced with poise and purpose. How their affection never smeared any scars in their minds and their endless kindness which helped the orphans to strive in existence of unheard and unspoken gratitude. He felt he couldn't betray them now when they needed him most and to derecognize the saga of epic motherhood they have showered on him. He felt he couldn't repay their efforts and embarrassments they must have faced in absence of male head of the family. He wanted to give them a peaceful solution to their long lived turbulent lives.

He was seriously considering their request or earnest desire and I was getting afraid of the repercussions of another shift of residence and another sequel of series of accommodations we would have to face after the decision. I was wondering how hard it would be to resettle with differences of climatic conditions, economic adjustments and difficulties of re-surfacing the obligations pending execution. While I was preoccupied by my own thoughts people were talking about the satellite telecommunication developments and the hazards of radio-activity they will be exposed to. They were discussing the invention of smart phones and internet revolution with which I was not much aware of. We were not going to die of cancer, rather we would be immunized and may die with other causes which were less painful. But in the end, nothing mattered. We were governed by our destined fates.

I was getting convinced that I can't possibly relate my growing concerns which are not dying down with passage of time and never letting me know what I was earlier. He has been committing the misdemeanor and violation of our faith extended in the relationship, and having done so all this long, now he was talking about 'my disclaimer or legal lingo', which is indicative of nothing short of his attempts of disgracing my intentions and assailing our marital decency.

UNDOCUMENTED DOCUMENTARIES

Doctor still has to stick to, the exchanged words, he still has to get some insights about his know how pressed for justifications, he still has to convey his presented values as concordant with happenings. What sort of benefits he has derived, what lessons he has learned, and because of the same what amount of loss incurred to us. We did not know anything, does he know that we want to know, after knowing the choices put in front of us. And I wanted to spend time in solitude for peace. I wanted to think about the happily spent times of the past, busy but joyful schedules, studies which were fun and advices received without reason. My pain ceases to end.

But time spent in North African Mediterranean coast was well spent. Once Doctor was put on special deputation to a secret military gathering among the revolutionary high command members in some distant desert resort, where I believe camps were installed for the meeting. They wanted a Doctor who should be of the same faith but not belonging to Arab race. There he was and felt obliged to go. It was a short visit of couple of days and he instructed his bachelor friends to take special care of me in his absence. Of course, he could not have carried me on that secret mission. I did not mind as it was a matter of couple of days.

Incidentally there was a desert storm and I suffered heat stroke, but his bachelor friends took good care of me. Extra care if I had to be truth full. They cooked meals for me and even were willing to feed me soups and drinks. Every few hours they took my axillary and sublingual temperature and gave me cold sponging. Cold sponging exceeded the requirements but they were trusted friends of Doctor. I thought probably it warranted swiping wet cloth over my arms, legs, back, chest and abdomen were all part of management. And I got well in a couple of days and Doctor returned to find me hale and healthy. I narrated the events to Doctor and he laughed aloud. 'Good thing they did not take your anal temperature'. Was all, he had to say. He was very liberal man in some matters.

I remember during our last visit to home country he returned back early and allowed more time for me to spend with family and friends. He had asked two of his friends with whom he used to share accommodation in the city before my marriage, to book my return flight with them. They obliged and as such his friends never used to take him lightly. As there was no direct flight and two stay overs in transit, his friends were carrying my luggage, helping in embarking and disembarking, paper works and transit stays in airline hotels. We were considered a group and allocated single room with large king size bed. They were particularly over protective in making me sit in the middle of three row seats and kept my mind busy in small talk, specially while take-offs and landing times.

They even did not mind my head resting on either of their shoulders in sleeping episodes, but they never leaned on me to avoid any discomfort. They probably knew my fears of thunderstorms and aviation. Both of them held my hands tenderly when we used to take off or land. One hotel provided us with a smaller room and a queen-sized bed, in which we were supposed to take rest. They took me in the middle and slept at the edge of the bed uncomfortably. Only once or twice while they were turning and tossing I was sandwiched but my elbows prevented excessive closeness. But they did not mind it and I had no reason to doubt their purpose. Moreover, I like the coziness and warmth in sleep and I was brought back safely in one piece and Doctor thanked them for their courtesy and concern. When I narrated the incidents of return journey, Doctor took it as small talk.

The purchasing capacity of local currency, namely 'Dinar' was high and livelihood cheap plus gifts of all kinds from fruits to meat in plenty brought in time before the refrigerator capacity allows some space. The block's ladies company was becoming friendlier and we used to exchange personal and private home lives and used to laugh and enjoy the gags. The gorgeous spinster was an equally interesting company always willing to be there for different kinds of needs. Once Doctor came early I was being massaged and he stood in the doorway watching with interest. Her slippery hands were caressing my body like an expert massage trainer, as were seen in spas for masseuses, but the exchanged sideways glances and subdued smiles between her and Doctor were not understood by me.

Doctor called his old-time friends from hometown and they were also a good company. Their wives became my thick friends as they joined services in different hospitals. I was surprised that the younger one had still to consume her marital relationships and the older one had specific time-based bedside contact with her husband as part of the deal. Both were thorough gentle man, including one specialist from northern sub-continent who was a surgeon but poor fellow could not get through with his wife and got separated. Here he became the most promising bachelor and nurses from our neighboring country were after him for attention and consideration for his second alliance. He was yet to finalize from so many, who were even taking liberties with him.

We used to go for city sight-seeing tours on tourism busses and used to have fun and giggles during the journey. The weekly off was fixed for Fridays and we used to have pot-luck kitty parties and relished them. There were Holy book's translation hour every week at our place and Doctor's friends used to come with kids. We planned for festival holidays and arranged barbeque parties. I learnt to feed both my kids and felt nice about it. The down town beach resting lounge with wooden seating were so relaxing that we used to watch sea gulls in the late evenings and cool breezes refreshing our body and mind. Visits to parks and gardens were a routine and I liked the greenery and loved the long drives.

I was serving my way, particularly to Doctor and humanity in general. I did it my way. I was not proud of it as, indeed I had less experience in pleasing Doctor specially. He was indeed older and more experienced. He discussed our problem to his lady colleague, another Doctor from Philippines and she suggested MJ techniques, but when I was told about the need of it, I was surely surprised. I asked my parking lot block's ladies and they said no harm and I gave my willingness with a lot of inquisitiveness. The lady Doctor came to our apartment and she was nice and pleasant to me. She even kissed at my cheeks both sides and appreciated the dimple which emerged on one. She must be aware of what she intended and dates and times were fixed according to everybody's convenience.

Doctor participated in those learning techniques as a student and I was a co-student. His sincere obedience to her instructions made me to follow suit. I was amazed and amused as they turned out to be different kind of exercises with lot of excesses in them. My willingness was not questioned neither lady Doctor's expertise not the wisdom of Doctor behind the need of it. If he thought they would help, then my willingness with or without consent becomes subsidiary. All went well and we noticed a lot of improvement in ourselves. The lady Doctor may be an expert but not very much experienced and she was perspiring herself at the end of sessions, which indicated lack of professionalism. But it did not matter, as we all were happy. I was happier than the Doctor and wanted more, but you cannot show too much of transference and Doctor also did not approve of my request for fear of counter transference.

My second pregnancy was progressing with no problems. I was at ease except for the facts this time the obstetrician was a male. His maneuvering my body was felt very different than the previous two pregnancies, I couldn't help it. There was this circuitous rotation of expatriate Doctors which was inevitable because of people going and people coming to that place. I was not supposed to sit cross legged and cross armed, instead there was too much of exposure involved and too many visits to the same person. My life was as such going in slow motion. Even if without enthusiasm I was being subjected to the routine. I admit I felt palpable sadness in me, in spite of pleasurable sensations. I was supposed to help shape the system to be more useful for people around. I thought I should be too pessimistic or optimistic about it. I remined steadfast and expected people to remain steadfast in their duties.

I was also obliged to leave an impact on the people. Impact for exaltation of the purpose behind it. My job had nothing to do with regulations, legislations or anything in particular. My job was to balance the differences among people to bring them to peace and tranquility of minds. I had to shape an attitude, a behavior, a culture which should bring some solace in the lives of the people. I had to relate to people to feel, touch, and embrace reality and get some benefit out of it. It was not my responsibility to stabilize the growing depreciation on economic basis, which can only have bubbles and more bubbles to pop out in the end. They are the by-products of our creations of havoc to self-destruction. Welcome to capitalist society, where globalization and technological advances had their roles to play, mostly turning out to devastation. No system yet developed to help the needy, except few lobbies and few segments of people.

The hypothetical basis of democracy with strings attached to foreign countries, developed and powerful, who are puppeteers dancing the puppets with the same strings. Only handful hold the authority to say, the rest to obey. We were left with a narrow passage through wisdom to squeeze stabilization of the system, joined with concepts and amendments of basic constitutions for opening up. I can't worry for them. I have to worry for Doctor and my children. They are my heart outside my body, jumping, playing, pumping and galloping and not caring about what is right and not. One can straighten out them easily and put them back in the chest for continued survival. Children should grow even if I have to shrink. Their growth is motivating to the society to bring balance in the system.

I should remain in my pockets and refuse to come out. It is always better to remain in the pockets and continue to work to train the new generation to become good leaders. Youth want to develop but doesn't know how and depend on guidance from elders. Guidance which is righteous and not misleading. Racism has initiated the turmoil. Silence had led to reversal of proceedings. I wanted retrieval of truth and success. It is persistence and sustenance of alienation from the existing system to a new system, which is more open and less covert and more selfless and less selfish. The difficulty may come with chances to be picked and directed to productive goals. Wisdom only has to sprinkle some stardust on the youth to guide them to progress. There were times I wanted to go back to my childhood and cajoling received by my mother, but Doctor always discouraged such thoughts, otherwise his self- respect and his own commitments would have prevented him for his longingness for me.

Off the record it was true and I had the best time of my life with Doctor. He was a thorough gentleman at times and could be certified for the same. I was lucky to have had him. He was caressing all possibilities for me other than those menial jobs of changing diapers, bathing children and holding them high and bring them down to listen to their giggles. He had always kept a distance in these rituals, but in all other matters he was an equal partner and maybe a better one. No, I was wrong at times, he was not an abuser, rather I had abused him at many occasions. I might have been raised that way. Doctor was very supportive and helpful in his typical unseen ways. He would make scrambled eggs and serve me with bread and butter. He would cook lunches and dinners and took me wherever I wished. He had one weakness and that was his inflated ego. He could justify it in arguments, debates or even rows. He was different in many ways.

I had my own weaknesses and fear of thunderstorms was just one of them, which he never bothered to treat or maybe he couldn't. He would allow me to commute with anybody, any time and anywhere. I knew he wouldn't mind my involvement in extra-marital affairs even. He was a different type altogether. Sometimes I thought of sharing him with my friends, as though he is relished cuisine to be shared. I was a docile person and people and I knew would crucify me if they come to know about it. I wondered why my expressions of experiences with his friends and acquaintances did not affect him. I told him about my pleasure in getting massaged by our gorgeous spinster neighbor and he casually said that he would witness it himself once. In his books 'every one is innocent, unless proved otherwise', as though innocence is a drug which would be declared toxic unless proved otherwise.

Doctor never hesitated to express the dark truth behind animate tendencies and dark secrets of human weaknesses. He would encourage me to talk to people, 'Don't consider it a hard task, as lessons will be learned from talking to people. And don't take it personally, rather take it as an experience with benefit and reward'. I also wanted to become a fighter, instead of becoming a victim and to struggle to survive. The humanity is clogging up with such learnings. People use bodies as amenities and for pleasure. But I want to push the laws prevailing to raise my voice against injustice and be ready for sacrifice, as I found the feeling of having sacrificed is more pleasurable than other things. People are crazy and the system governing them is crazy. I shouldn't be afraid to get labelled as feminist.

Only of late women were given voting rights and only after fighting for their cause. Women fought for equal job allocations, dependent upon the population ratio. What a system, and how many flaws I could rectify. Homosexuality was legalized but why military service still banned them from entry. There is a need for commitment of social change and a complete one. Business flourishes by making boys toys rough and crude and girl toys fragile and delicate. It was the root cause of the problem. People were allowed their whims and fancies to provide elegant toys with discrimination for their in-depth desire for discrimination. No lady president has yet been elected as the executive head of the greatest country, America with its so called liberal points of view.

I will get justice for women all around the world. I know this culture will get ruined. This society will take its last breath. It is like continuing to work even if you are not being paid for. Pass on slogans that women are empowered. 'But you are also supposed to regard the conduct of the pursuit'. Doctor always used to say. There are always two sides of the coin, picture, jury or justice. I will hesitate to light candles and march against domestic violence. I may have challenges greater than this, but my work will be admired sometime, if not now, in defense and not in offence. People may say I am doing it for own glory but it will not discourage me. I cannot control other's thinking. I should keep my poise and learn from Doctor's speeches or whispers.

I have to keep in mind that people respect success and not failures. I am not facing a generation gap, as this was going on since ages. I cannot also have a win-win situation, as that would be expecting too much. Failures are important part of learnings. I was like a prophet without honor in my own household. And change will take years to internalize the need of it, but it will take place. Changes will be gradual and they have to be welcomed. No urgency depicted and no flooding required for a change. I should not expect it that way. It will be suicidal attempt to blast this society, impending a slow death.

PRAGMATIC ANECDOTE

Doctor, told me so many words. 'You may note that such programming of unwanted changes piles up into frustrations and invite traps in long term routine and examples need not be quoted here. The results of such manipulations intended or not is nurturing and mentoring skills into inaccessible vaults and elimination of anything productive or gainful'. I made him to understand that there was a time when he appeared talented, exceptional, ostensibly forecasting progress and achievement but now things appear different. Now he was persuaded by irrelevancies and influenced by incongruities and not expected of any accomplishments.

They are not worth anymore to commit them to our memories and in the end, we should be better off not knowing them, we would prefer refraining ourselves from knowing them rather knowing them should be slammed as good riddance. We are still to face repercussions of introductions with his formed opinions about us, about me more importantly, more so that he believe in dictating terms, that he want to control the situations and that our presented circumstances are not worth more than junk mail to be strewn in gutters.

I was qualified but did not know how to present it. I also knew that my options are thinning out with passage of time. Here they were. To expect me and believe in what Doctor has said. I had not got involved with him for so long to hear it, that I am a weed growing in the backyard to be neglected and forgotten or to be removed. I didn't know what exactly he was proud of. It can't be a miracle. A miracle in these times is a mis-spoken word. It is not merely a sixer from a fluke shot in cricket or a goal by a self-turning ball from a corner of soccer game. It also can't be a hit and run accident, which has not been recorded in the police files. Anything can happen with these scenes except a miracle.

What the hell I was in the middle of the winter night. It could have been a stolen car meant for a cold-blooded plan for murder to appear as a man slaughter, to get away with. There are no games, no shows, Champaign bottle corks flying around, no nothing, except our reputation or some misquoted statements. I am not a prophet to show miracles.

I am a janitor to carry people up and down in a hurry. The math involved was simple. Easy to solve the equations. Easy to clean up the trash. Easy to erase the mistakes, easy to recognize and easy to forget. There were several channeled dramas but no lines to be remembered, released or replayed. Immortal friends, immortal foes or immortal non-existent shadows and nothing real. I am a jack of all but master of none.

I am a partner with a designation of a wife, innocently simple and simplicity at its core. I don't have any time frames, ant dead lines to work against and I haven't made any program to live by. I had my modest suggestion, passing on with religious regularity to Doctor all these years of living together. It was natural of fondness to develop during this time. It comes out spontaneously out of the blue. There were no vanities of do's and don'ts to come up with. It had a substantial value of its own. I have to analyze the dimension of the problems we share and get hold of opportunity to magnify the flaws to suit my needs, my choices, my likes and my dislikes. Now within my jurisdiction later to be outsourced. With all that was going on, it was difficult to keep a balance delicately poised between pleasures and business, a shifting balance that I had been trying to divide within myself all along. The real balance comes when I start enjoying what I am doing.

I remained on borderlines and couldn't move up to straighten out the balance. It is always challenging initially but later, one could get stabilized on a foundation, to rise above and construct oneself. I was taught that I should be ready to stall, stalk, de-stabilize the opportunities for an advantage. It was a tough decision to make and even tougher to execute it. But the time had come, so I took a fresh breath of air, cleansed my impurities to make myself ready to stand the tests of the time. I had no complaints whatsoever with my life. We went on vacations, once stayed in UAE, found Dubai better than any place. Doctor purchased some jewelry and elegant clothing for me. We stayed in best hotel and served well. Hotel was providing spa facilities, masseuses and what ever asked for.

During another visit to home land we stayed in Karachi, met Doctor's relatives, exchanged pleasantries and had a good time. He introduced me to his cousin sister who was to get married to him, a three-dimensional beauty, if chances were met with in time. He also introduced me another cousin sister who was barren and wanted his child to be harbored. His elderly relatives were very kind and loving and caring type. The city was overcrowded with colorful taxis and auto-rickshaws. The weather was humid and tropical and I sweated a lot and drank a lot. I didn't want to be nursed again for any more heat strokes to receive cold sponging's. they always made me feel embarrassed and humiliated having been taken care of by deprived bachelors, even if they were Doctor's friends. I carried special dresses with me and gifts too. We were well received and parted with sorrow laden hearts.

Therapeutically all went well but for those introductions which were casually done leaving me to peel my own skin. I can't admit it was dishonesty but too bluntly presented and too tenderly perceived. I could have been angry yelling out aloud, but after repetitive small talks, elaborate diplomacy and anxieties piling up to heaps of worries I left it for some other time. I had to defend my reputation of simplicity, modesty and humbleness. No. it maybe a witty attempt of humor, which kids use to kid around. I was trying not to think too ambitiously. I have to live years and decade of my life still. I can try to avoid exposing my secrecies to public, but I am not answerable to Doctor's interpretations. It is like selection of right answer from a multiple-choice questionnaire. Life is still beautiful and I shouldn't trade it against my formed opinions. I must revise my conclusions.

It is nothing but a deficiency of some neuro-transmitters, created out of some hormone deficiencies, causing chemical imbalance and had to be supplemented. How does it matter now? It is like a lens I am looking through and suddenly everything is turned upside down. As such nothing from the past can be brought to the present or carried to future. We can not pick from where we last left. I should do me a favor, get out, carry a treasure map and start digging from my backyard. I cannot talk about withholding anything from Doctor, he can uphold his triumph card whenever he likes. I communicated to him that it is not nostalgia we are talking about, we are talking about realities of life. Ground realities. 'You are good at what you do, advice from your insights, guidance from your introspection and bring out to surface your greatness, but you will stick to it and do not change, be your original self'.

He made a position for himself, a place for himself and he cannot withdraw, as he is drawn into it with my life. So, he cannot get lost. It became a nightmare, I couldn't figure out the reasons, the whole concept got changed for me. The crap nobody else got into. I am going to bind him, bind him to do what is legible and what is reasonable, leave alone the pre-requisites. Sometimes I have to take decisions on some delicate subjects before they merge into other subjects. They will become your meal ticket for survival. It is not easy to get re-assured. Nobody has to tell me what to do or what not to do. I should leave things where they are. Leave it that way. It is not a cancer, which we can clean with a broom stick. Shortly I will be reminded of my wisdom.

Welcome home. The stay was busy, busy like a train station. The imposed restriction becoming little overwhelming at times. I was trying to gather my thoughts before they get broadcasted. No thought insertion, no thought broadcast, no thought interception, no nothing. They are plain simple meaningless thoughts. I do think but I have to bring some precision into them. That should be the goal. I wanted to address it to Doctor, 'Listen to me, like an obedient child, like a nut, or a cracker, but just don't wrap around your arms over me to embrace for re-assurances. Your assurances are not like hall of fame or a piece of art. I can't make myself an easy prey to them and I can't see through them'.

'I have to find someone who could see through translucencies. Transparencies are easy, but you are not transparent and you don't keep things transparent. Your intentions are a mirage to me. The inappropriateness of my thoughts could bring a response, could charge a relevance and see a determination of criteria of conservation of our relationship. Your understanding is much too dangerous than the high voltage sign of a skull with crossed long bones. So, let's have a malignant bond and a round of applause for keeping you happy all this long'. It all seemed to be an unanticipated cultivation of small farm, with immediate cost-benefit ratios to be formed. I will use both words unanticipated and immediate in the same sentence. These words are significant to cause tissue change if consumed.

His dramatization of self-designation and effective attention seeking attitude had made him to see what I think and made him to interpret what I do, hence he thought I had made it written by someone else and had copy pasted it for him. It is quite clear that he was guilt ridden of his misdeeds and got easily provoked. Beyond doubt I have mortified all human values and offended our social status and formal relationships, by anticipatory apprehension that we intend to go for justice one day. Grinning to myself I closed the door locked it from inside. I was to myself. The house looked tidy and clean. The carpets maybe changed in near future. Our apartment was on the third floor and walking up was cumbersome. The top floor bugged me when I had to carry groceries up, but it was sort of exercise to justify skipping a gym membership, which was non-existent at that place. Doctor had been comfortable with contentment with what we had and very occasionally tended to return to his grim face.

There were, and are now, several misunderstood concepts including my knowledge of legacies called upon him, like mode of transfer of funds, exchanged mail communications, his obvious cunningness in equaling the proof of commitments being vague, allowing him to escape the liabilities, etc., etc. His frequent change in tactical measures, being vindictive at times and threatening at other times also indicated gross deviation in his thinking and behavior, but firstly his misinterpretation of facts, that we are looking into websites for legal frivolities, which is now clear was done by him, not warranting my choice or preference, as he was the defaulter and not me.

But some recollections kept haunting. Why he showed me my picture of the beach with beige color dress and when I shouted at him by saying that where has my dress gone, he stated that I am wearing it and when I complained why it is not evident, he protested with words like it is not his fault. I grabbed the picture from his hand and he jovially mentioned that he intends to enlarge it. The curious exchanges of glances and smiles with the gorgeous spinster nurse and he were questionable but I hesitated to explore for the year of disclosure that the scenes were intended to be repeated in between both of them. He was cautious in his disclosures he already informed me that when ever he had returned back early from his vacation that girls were there to look after him.

Turning on lights and pulling off my layers of clothing, instead of putting kettle on stove I moved into bathroom and started bathing keeping the door open. I felt I am not a wife with kids and does not have the luxury of decision making. Doctor was to join me later but I got a feeling that unless he kept secrets tighter than the vaults of 'Revolutionary high command', I found it hard to believe that any other woman would voluntarily cohabit with a man like him. There wasn't any hard-pressed need in the world to put up with that level of stress. My mind temporarily shortened at that point. I curled up on the couch, wedging a cushion under the small of my back, I thought about my will and pleasure to remain with him for the rest of my life. My diary was an inch away from my big toe and I decided to postpone the writing part for the time being. It sounded as though life is business as usual.

CIRCUMSTANCIAL
INCRIMINATIONS

Doctor manipulated the integrity of relationship between family emotions and jeopardized our peace of mind by his arrogant viciousness, doubting my sincerity by announcing intentions of denial about any dues and here he may note and register in his IQ that this and all details of the present deal was in my knowledge, which even made me to ask the same is taking place at his end. He kept thrusting his mischief and exploited my innocence and played with my believing nature to his advantage, which subjected me to enormous discomfort and to unforeseen repercussions, instead he may hold the situation till elders sort out this ambiguity brought now by his detrimental mental state and not earlier than this transaction. So, do not test my guarded deceit less arrangement, which as of now cannot overshadow his callousness and had already caused me enough mental anguish, which even warrants some compensation from his side.

Marriages are marriages, all the same with minor deviations and small alterations. No one has to look back and pass judgements or form any pre-conceived notions. First few years is struggles in adjustments and knowing the ins and outs. The following few years will be good, fun and achievements. The next few years will remain satisfactory and the following few years not satisfactory but one gets used to the lifestyles and mode of interactions. LIving with ups and downs, hot and cold relationships, rows and embraces and so on and so forth. One has to get used to it, to take it to the end. One can get so used to it that any deviation may upset the balance, disturb the harmony and harass the individuals involved. Like people get used to imprisonment, immaterial of they being culprits or innocents and remain there for rest their lives. I read somewhere that out of 1.3 million prisoners about 130,000 are innocent victims of the flaws of the system.

The system of law enforcement with the intricacies of the judicial system governed by corrupt politicians, corrupt lawyers and corrupt executives. To add to my suffering, I also read that the worst among them is the system conforming the police ignorance, police negligence, police jeopardy, police hatred, police brutality, inefficiency and insufficiency. I am sorry about these great systems of these great countries, great nations and great races they are governed with. I cannot absorb anymore. I should stop worrying about. I should focus on my success story. Success has a set criterion of measurement, Doctor would agree with me. He made me successful, he managed my paucity of time for success, better still was the fact that he never made me feel how time passes by and that is a success in itself. I had total faith in him to deserve my success.

I felt as though I met an angel in the form of a mortal and while walking barefooted in the wet grass imagining my poetic phrases of my diary or journal which I had written for him. That made me to recollect whether I had shown my writings to him, if not then it is not too late. I searched my diary and found it. I opened it and noticed Doctor's scriptures from where I left. They consumed the pages in local dialect which I was familiar with. I started reading. All of them were undated and short. They contained the thoughts perceived by him at different times and recorded for documentation. He never had the problem of passing times. He must have felt the need to document and he did.

The words were legible and meaningful. They said addressing to me, as it was my diary and meant or me and understandably he has seen it and ascribed some replies.

My love,

Your indifference towards me left me with no option other than finding an escape from my feeling which would mean a strategy to forget the emptiness of my heart. Your beauty remained possessive of me and your memory will not fade from my mind. Those were equivalent to dooms day for me, through which I had passed alone amidst misery and sorrow that I did not live to die or die to live for you. My love for you is religious value of my faith in your innocence and openness which you should try to peep in and see for yourself. They are full of my desires for your belongingness, which I fear may remain as my wishful thinking alone someday, but I don't want or wish it that way.

Other than your looks of grace and delight, there is nothing left for me to enjoy any spring or blossoming of flowers, as to me gardens are blooming due to the dew drops which have fallen from your fragrant hair curls. What I was assuming did not match my expectations and heart broke out for you scattered in pieces wanting you to reassemble for my life to go on, otherwise I will live a dead life mourning my own death which did not get harvested by your sown fruits to be reaped.

My life will extinguish like an evening which is quivering with its own sorrow to convert soon into the moonlit night which will demand your company for my solitude, rest assured by nature's springs. Then only those ambitious wants of innumerable people craving for attention will be heard and I would lose my grip on the slippery hands of yours which once I could hold onto to my satisfaction and solace.

Your scarf covering like half hiding your beauty in veil, the border staying back on your dimpled cheek appeared lighting the gray shades with colors depicting eternal bliss for me. For a glimpse of your tantalizing beauty, I find hidden thousands of joys of paradise and the glamour of your looks which is desired by me hides millions of happy cajoling and unaccountable temptations which are subdued under your feet are belligerent under the dust.

Every look of your proverbial curves which attract the youthful yearning of everyone. Your gorgeous body, whose imagination itself is electrifying and the bidding to reach and hold it are thirsty to quench their pent-up wishes, which will never end the gratifications of anyone's needs. Your graceful gait can be sacrificed over innumerable recognitions of walks and the glow of your skin can be sacrificed over several emerging rainbows in the sky.

Your black curls of stray hair carry the pleasures of crowded feelings for all, are as though long nights of separation are ending into pleasing expectations of union. Your eye's exquisiteness made by nature is stimulating the nature itself with a pride and honor and the poetic verses failing in expression of the prettiness they possess in them.

Your voluptuous body can feel glared by the dress which is worn to get admired by the costume for appraisal and admiration. The trees and gardens may yearn for closeness and to find a reason to bow down their respects in your adoration and I happened to stroll through these captivating conditions created by your presence and I felt attracted to your innocence and grace.

Now this path has evidently become a permanent glory for love seekers and admirers of beauty and causing heart-warming elegance and satiety of unfulfilled hunger for them. The breezes which brush past your contours get scented by your fragrance which is intoxicating to me and the space around you is whispering soft spoken words in your appreciation, which I alone could hear.

Ultimately your mystifying soul which is lodged near me is about to convert into a place of prostration in your loveliness, which for me is to stay and recall all those past days during which I was flattered by your company. I feel compelled to take the cozy shade of your shadow for my incomparable desires to embrace it and the sleep laden half-closed eye shades, lined by black eyeliner, which haunt me for your longingness.

Your ecstatic dignity of poise which carry with your charm is filled and empowers me as a slave for your shapely arms scripted with blue veins tortuous in their run, are a source for me to visualize your presence and are the jest of my poetic verses which can never end to glorify your appearance. My artistic needs and requirements are insufficient to describe your charisma and world circumvolute around your figure for ever. Your stunning looks will never rest in my want for you and my restless soul will continue asking for your favors, which you had been showering on me all along.

My flow and stream of thoughts and feelings will remain thirsty for your closeness and companionship, which is adorable for all but a privilege for me. Is it your call from your wet lips and the taste which seems unsatisfying for all times, I will explore from where I could get approximation to the same and I will wait to hear the sound of melodies which are lingering in the space calling for me?

You have always managed to suit yourself with your beauty, but I wish and pray you don't get pride in it, as it is a blessing God gifted and I want you to remain grateful and thankful for all that has been provided to cherish. It is time you admire God's creation in your form and texture and adore His continued support to maintain it. I did not realize until now that you had been waiting for me and caring me and in your glances.

I had found a world of understanding for my shortcomings and handicaps and now I console me that underneath my desire to share my dreams with you, you managed to carry me away to seven heavens through my imaginations and provided me with everything in this era and in this time and held me in embrace tightly in your arms, not to let me go away, which I doubt I deserve.

You seem to be grieving for your losses and got captivated by your whimsical obsessions over long grieved losses, which I can recognize and identify. It is your separation from me for short lived stances, your separation anxiety associated with it. But you are not alone who were missing grateful people who were helped and healed by you. Their problems remedied. You may be missing out on your colleagues and friends of scholastic wisdom, who used to part their advices to you, your useful and gainful preoccupations of time which might have brought a sense of solidarity and satisfaction.

I know your position and commands which are lacking in this time are equally great losses for you. Your qualifications and the cures which you have implanted on the needy and deserving are not available to you overseas, where materialistic gains over valued your mental gratifications, all being the rewards of cumulative benefits you have earned by hard work and sincere honesty towards duties and responsibilities. You will be rewarded for your efforts and results.

Your admirer

I was getting more comfortable with life. We never had fans installed or felt the need of it. The Mediterranean climate was a boon to us. We would need heaters in the winters and felt warm and convenient under quilts. Winters always used to arouse me and Doctor liked it on need-based closeness. I used to take advantage after he sleeps soundly and put my face on his chest to hear his occasional wheezes, a product of chronic smoking. There were no smoke alarms in the apartments and his thick blue pipe smoke was also starting to stimulate me. Children were happy and had plenty of toys to while away time. Doctor also used to play with them in his spare time.

Once I found my younger son a thin frail boy, toddler still missing even after a thorough search. I got worried and cried. Doctor returned early by chance and I ran down to inform him about the missing child even before he came out of his car. He kept his calm and carried me inside and asked me to look under the bed to find him sleeping on the carpet. Then I saw my daughter in his cradle and later came to know that out sibling rivalry she has thrown him down and out of her once owned cradle and slept inside peacefully. On recollection of the scene I couldn't resist the urge to laugh and laughed aloud. Doctor hugged me and notified not jump to any assumptions, leave alone conclusions before getting rest assured about the facts.

We were happy but on the contrary the nation was decaying, people were degenerating and our resourcefulness weakening, perhaps our assets have been exhausted or faded in the dust. I will be there helping out with recovery. I told Doctor in particular, when he was not around. No one will get any rhetoric from me other than him. Over a brief moment I feel liable for these agnostic realisms for him. Now he also has to prepare for the expected unforeseen migration back to adversaries and un-assigned tasks which are awaiting our return.

I feel partly responsible for these awaited calamities and I feel I am as capable as before to shoulder his burdens from him. I looked every now and then at the clock hanging on the wall to avoid seeing the frozen hands which should move at their regular speed and don't let me feel the brunt of passing time. I still allure him and want to be with him, as before and part with a helping hand as much as I could do to lessen his weight.

Back home the system will kill us, the infrastructure will injure us, the inadequacies will haunt us, the wild fire of corruption will taunt us, the imbalance of power and the struggle will hurt us. There the rich are becoming richer and the poor poorer, but we will remain contended with what we had and what we will get. I know his priorities and I respect them. We will not suffer much as we have each other to console and infect confidence to fight for our rights.

Let the system take a downhill course, let the culture ruin itself, let the greedy get transient relief. We will bring control on these deviations and take it as a bold declaration from me, refueled by energy to face the unexpected. I have a feeling I could help. Selective honesty will not get us anywhere. Selective sincerity is never sufficient to learn the truth. These words should be erased from the dictionary, as they have only theoretical value and lack practical benefits.

WISHFUL DESIRES

Doctor decided to carry me to introduce his faculty members, before our intended return from North Africa. I was pondering about the need, but he knew the reasons and I was supposed to yield to his plans. Leave alone whims and fancies. Out of his colleagues I was only introduced to that Philippian lady Doctor, who used to visit our place for some purposeful help for us to learn and for her to rehearse. She liked me for sure, but I was not equally sure about her likewise. I always wonder about those who are not aware of those methods, as to how they get along and are they being deprived of their rights. One thing was sure that, it did no harm to us. We would have learned them with experience and time. I whole heartedly agreed to visit his hospital and promised myself not to be an ill-tempered or ill-mannered diva. It was my obligation to help in all means towards his efforts which up till now had been honest and useful or fruitful for the family. Our unit especially.

I didn't know the local dialect and may feel out of place, was my concern. A silly thought crossed my find that he should have swapped another girl as his wife and introduced her to them. It followed another ridiculous thought that swapping of partners should have been allowed in our culture for specific reasons. The locals were cordial and the director of his hospital was hospitable. He bowed down to greet me and took my hand and kissed it. He also must have mistaken me for a Princess of some godforsaken dynasty of some state in south Asia. I felt his tip of the tongue over my knuckles. I was careful to manage my feelings of overblown importance. Not that I didn't like it, but it was not the time to reverberate any emotions. One more kiss on my hand from another male would have blown me apart.

I was keeping my good manners, no matter with whom I was dealing. I was polite as usual but I was not a saint. A kiss on the dorsum of hand with a flip of tongue on the knuckles cannot keep any human a saint. There were other colleagues who were occupied in different sort of discussions with Doctor in local dialect, in which he was fluent. His language and slang could hardly differentiate him with any other local. Some juniors were even debating the deferred diagnostics of some patients. One good looking lady intern brushed shoulders with Doctor and took his side, to remain there. The introductions didn't take long. We moved in the administrative building but I was not shown the in-patient wards. I was not eager as well. I was not the president of a country to expect my life size portrait there.

I wanted to return in urgency, even if it is going to be my last visit. I remember the earlier visit, when some function took place, I saw some people but from some distance, moreover I was not concentrating on faces, then. I had brought my girl child in some fancy-dress show, made up as a nurse with a thick white paper cap, typical of nurse's wear clipped into her bushy hair curls. There were some other nationality kids wearing white loose T shirts and stethoscope hanging in their necks fancy-dressed as Doctors. Well it was fun. There were other cultural programs of other nationality and grown up nurses who danced and sang songs, very unfamiliar sounding. One full bodied Sudanese nurse attempting to dance in a rhythmic way was appealing until she caught herself in her 8 feet chiffon Saree cloth tail and fell down on the stage, not able to synchronize with the drums and she fell upside down, with her legs protruding out of the lower open portion and appeared penetrating like thumb nails after manicure.

That day we collected lot of gifts and today we collected lot of smiles. I had a quick fuse off and didn't know how to conduct myself among Arabic speaking people, experts in their fields. I should have learnt Arabic or should have taught how to absorb piercing looks and material damage. I was repeating single phrase every now and then, 'Peace be upon you' and 'Thank you', of course in Arabic language. My companion looked no different in their company than the rest. He was speaking local dialect in local slang fluently and I started counting 100 backwards. I was sure at the count of 10 I will leave the premises. I was wearing our traditional costume which appeared little too tight and little too short for my size. The necklace sparkling around my neck and ear rings, moon shaped hanging and dangling in my sides, with every nod I was making of my head.

We shook hands in the end and mine was becoming little slippery with every other grip. But the exchange was affectionate and blessings passed on were sincere. The director looked back and I smiled back repeating the same phrases. I felt no excitation or attraction in his rugged face. He had kissed my hand like a primary school boy does or taught to do so, as a Victorian mannerism and becomes shy to act like one. Doctor appreciated my personality.

'You were looking great'. He continued, 'And you acted well, there should have some camera flashes to capture your image and style on celluloid'.

I wondered as to why he complimented me, as he usually refrains himself from doing so. The rest of the return journey was in silence, except that he asked me to remind him, next day about the pending work of the RTA case which was in court.

It so happened, I recollected that we were riding our newly purchased Toyota car, a corolla model of gray color and it was fast turning from twilight stage to darkness of night and we were practically speeding, with kids in the back seat. We were occupied in small talk discussing about our future and our kids. Suddenly I gave a high-pitched scream, more suited for an air raid signal, as I saw a shadow crossing the road. It was a stray cat, which appeared in front of our car from side lane. Doctor applied brakes, over and above the noise coming from the radio of local folk music. The car tires screeched to halt and we heard another loud thump and a jolt at the rear, which was another car from the back hitting our rear fender, while the driver following us tried arduously to jam his brakes and hit us at the rear side. The noises which followed were that of shattering glass of the headlights bulbs. The driver in the rear was a retard using his reflexes sluggishly.

We were still and it started to rain. Our head lights throwing double silvery rays which were still on and a police man approached from nowhere and even shot some snaps. The arguments among male voices lasted few minutes while the case was booked in our favor and referred to court for damage claims. The fault always lies with the driver at the back, who was supposed to maintain a distance. I immediately realized my mistake because cats in town being struck with hit and run accidents was a common affair on roads, more so at nights. The other driver showed me his flexed middle finger while rushing passed my side and vanished from the sight. I felt embarrassed probably against his judgement and mind of a crazy drug addict.

My gaze moved to side and then to the rear, while Doctor inspected the damage to our car. I was willing to bet our strong and broad bumper must be clean and unscratched. Doctor's lips pursed into a silent whistle and he folded the slip of paper into his pocket and he drove and moved on. His face looked like he was ready to garrote someone with his side chain for the specs. His eyebrows frowned upon the partiality of the police man. My lips sticky with gloss tasted of synthetic strawberry. The smile on Doctor's lips was ridiculously fake, but the matter had to be forgotten as the case was closed for another hearing at the local court. I heard some murmurings from the back seat where children were still sleeping in their chairs. I felt like a girl friend on dating experience in her spare time of mother Teressa.

The moods were spoiled. The damage claim was a tedious process consuming time and exertion. His mood became dispassionate than what it was an hour before. We reached home in silence, while the local folk song was still making noise, but with lower volume. I think he had other matters to think and to attend. He may even be considering options of research in his faculty. He had already published scientific articles in international journals. He probably wanted more to publish or he was weighing the pros and cons of his intended plan to return to his home country to be of some service to his mothers. Even after reaching home he was still in deep thinking. I loved his expression when he thinks gravely, more so when he is lost in his thoughts. I touched him tenderly.

Back inside our apartment Doctor realized with his crossed fingers entwined that I could notice the change and felt the need to reassure me that it is nothing worrisome. He released his finger's grip and cupped my face.

'I love you', I sprouted.

He smiled. 'Me too, more this year than before, more this week than last month, more today than yesterday, more now than an hour before'. His usual way of responding.

'I am concerned about the implications of my decision on you and I can't comprehend whether I would continue loving you like this way, later'. He mentioned casually.

I lifted my hand and laid it over his, trying to link my fingers into his. That was a romantic side of Doctor, which is showered on me occasionally. I tended to ease out his tensed-up muscles. His restless fingers needed to calm down. He flicked over his notepad to check on the coming week's schedule.

I noticed fine tremor of his fingers and I sat down beside him on the sofa. He eyed my portrait on the mantel and smiled. Ironically but silently I became restless. I came closer to him. His strong side was an assuring touch to my thigh. Knowingly he refused to worry on the pending stamping of the exit procedures on the passport, I was aroused and continued caressing his thigh. The maneuvers which followed continued some quite some time until we both were relaxed and we slept in relaxed postures, with our bodies entwined this time. The next day was its usual routine, except that it was his off day from work. I knew by now the methodology of resuming normalcy. I was beginning to understand how to normalize him.

His reputation was equally enormous in expressing his care and concern and love. I felt like wearing the same beige color dress and to get drenched in water for another snap. I told him in so many words. He was smart in these unspoken words. I allowed him to pull me closer against his body and this was my gesture for his ill flattered sociopathic glory. I heard kids crying for hunger. I bottled up next feeds and gave them. They swallowed in whole and slept again. I also noticed that the morning as very bright and sunny and equally refreshing to my urges. We played with each other for the following hour and slept again. Doctor woke when he heard kid's voices, fully awake. Our day passed in the same repetitive rituals.

Not that I was fed up waiting for cargo ships for utilities and amenities to be un-loaded or friends, genuine friends notifying to each other as to where, a particular need is made available, neither I was tired of sewing or knitting sweaters for growing kids, which other ladies of the block were still doing as pastime. But I was definitely getting waxed by formalities of festivals. Embraces which were tighter and warmer. I sometimes thought they are trying CPR techniques to refresh their cordiality into their memoirs. I felt like laughing without getting entertained. I knew Doctor doesn't believe in performances only, on or off stage, rather he strongly believed in execution of duties in a methodical way. With passage of time I was becoming fond of him, but in spite of having lived so long with him, I didn't know whether the feeling is reciprocal.

It was unfortunate that one day after strolling in the parking lot, I returned and sneaked through the key hole of the main door for no reason. I saw Doctor and our gorgeous spinster together in the living area. Doctor was motionless and she was trailing leisurely. He then gripped her face in his hands tightly with out pulling. She brought her mouth closer to his. They sat curled together for long minutes. Their noses, I think were touching each other's, lips faint distance apart, their breaths must be mingling and her eyes were lit up with some kind of light.

I heard her say, 'Does it make you feel any better'.

Doctor looked blankly at her trying to understand what she meant. I wonder whether he was also thinking how I may react if I am witnessing the scene, while I was actually witnessing it at that moment. I remembered Doctor had already told me that our neighbor looked after him in my absence or late joining, after vacations. I kept things to myself to encounter some other time.

I was in no mood for a talk, an argument, a row, a fight or whatever. I was in no mood to perpetuate debate, explanation, a justification or even bad news print or press media for myself. I need not be rude to anyone in particular. As far as Doctor is concerned, he is hard to be tolerated. I recalled some of my girl-friends from school time who were difficult people and difficult to be tolerated. No doubt he was not involved in any romantic scandal of recorded cheating case. I also doubted the hint of no hesitation if a chance is provided to him served with garnishing on a plate. I was happy knitting sweaters for kids. My girl had cuter looks and fluffy curls of hair, which could be easily messed with by neighboring boys of her age, as they used to come in hold easily. She would cry for help; other ladies would remain indifferent and I would boil in myself.

They should give proper training to their kids to behave properly. Proper behaviors are wanted norms of a society. Good thing Doctor never had the time or chance to witness such dramas. I knew he wouldn't tolerate. One has to have a thick skin to bear with such mediocracies or silly presentations. I notified the fact to our neighbor lady and interestingly she started imagining how he would be with her in bed. I choked again at the thought and hurt my finger with the needle with which the sweater being knitted. He may not be faithful, but I cannot make my body from waist down numb and let the faults of companions be ignored.

'He is a bit of a dish to relish', she added.

She should have known our chemistry. I vaguely feared contamination by a neighbor woman, lady or not.

I wanted to change the subject, before I get into a stirring lust for Doctor. I was his game and not the neighbor women, even if someone's contours are more impressive than me. He is my game only. Why should women folk usually like their kids and other's husbands. I made a murmuring sound, dismissing the imagination to go any further. Any more than what is required. I thought I better moan and complain and then run away. Doctor may be adorable but not for others. He was meant for me and me alone. I could share him with broadmindedness or whole heartedness.

FICTITIOUS FACTS

It was good that we planned to go home, home country. Let's see when and how it shapes up. How much I may miss Doctor at odd times. I felt like tripping from where I stood. My opinion of women having vicious taste for other men gives a low profile and low vision imperfection. I didn't have to be jealous of other women having better shapes and better partners. I was told in the parking lot by a senior lady that men don't sleep with other women until they care about them, immaterial of the gratification they get or not. All this was wisdom to me, which in Doctor's books would be plain simple stupidity. The life otherwise moved on with invitations to birth day parties, get togethers of friends, Doctor's embassy deputation works and so on.

My daughter's birth day party was a success. All friends and their families participated, the entire function was video graphed and the grand event was saved on celluloid tape. In spare time friends used to bring home country's movies on VCR cassettes, which used to be circulated for everybody's benefit. Films were watched late night on Thursdays, to allow us late risings and late brunches. Doctor's contacts used to bring us consumables like meat, chicken, eggs and fruits to the extent that we couldn't store them and necessitated cutting portions for distributions, increasing popularity but it was part of duty to share and feel better.

Once a very costly piece of jewelry was boxed and given to me at the door by an acquaintance with a card denoting the sender, but the sheer cost of the pearl studded golden jewelry made us to return it to the owner, of course with thanks. Doctor anyhow gave a favorable report to him. While all the routine activities were taking place, we were also planning and preparing for our intended return. All discouraged us but commitments were made and they had to be met with. The detailed program and the eventualities were to be finalized and approved by God. I proved to be the last person to diet strictly, but somehow the energy output over weighed the energy intake and I was getting slimmer. It didn't really matter to Doctor how 'Hour glass like' I have become. What was important for him was health and fitness.

The next week was Doctor's night call duty and he returned unusually late. Otherwise he used to return in small hours of the morning, but that day he came late, so late that our gorgeous spinster was already in our home preparing breakfast in the kitchen. Incidentally she was wearing the same night down as that of mine. She used to do such casual visits often. I was still rolling in bed and kids were asleep. I knew she is in the kitchen and I always liked her company in the mornings. Doctor entered the kitchen mistook her for me and grabbed her from behind. She didn't give any startled response, which indicated to me about the fact that she was accustomed to such embraces. Doctor always remain in good moods at the end of call duty. He was about to lift her that I summoned courage to call him from bed room.

They were caught in surprise and so was I. He looked back at her and the way she glanced triggered a cautious spark of optimism. I didn't know how he felt but it was a step up for that morning. I knew she must have smelled men's after shave fragrance and was ready to put her arms around him. Both refrained and parted without a comment. I interrupted him by enquiring about the calls and he went into too much attention to detail about his work. He groomed his finger through my hair. I was pleased for his sake. I didn't want to spoil his mood. I couldn't behave my own fallibility. He pulled on my ear lobe and caressed my cheek with dimple appearing gracefully for his solace. I pressed my palm against his chest and felt his heart throb. The spinster had left by then understandably and we had all the time to ourselves before kids would complete their sleep and wake up.

The sudden second deputation of Doctor to oil field was un warranted, uncalled for and un-welcomed. He was supposed to relieve the Doctor who was on extended leave and the on-duty Doctor insistent on going for vacation. There was no question of refusal as the orders from the Minister was an obligatory verdict passed against our program, plans and wishes. But I believe it was going to be short deputation. How short or how long was immaterial, in comparison to Doctor's liking. He just didn't like the climate of desert, with frequent desert storms and lack of amusement other than passing time within the male company of employees in his spare time. The visibility sometimes getting reduced to one-meter distance and the food made by the cooks difficult to swallow, because of pure Arabic cuisines and bland dietary preparations.

He allocated his bachelor friend placed temporarily in the drawing room to take care of my needs and he left in a hurry. His friend was a decent young man with courteous behavior and caregiving attitude. He would drive us in the evenings and get us all wants from the super markets. He was jocular and cracked jokes so funny that I couldn't resist laughing. He would play with kids in his spare time and also attend to his duties. He would collect mail from our post box and do the laundry of all our clothes. I used to feel little embarrassed, when he would separate his clothes from ours and try folding the dried bras and panties. He was a good company in Doctor's absence and used to relish my cooked food. Doctor kept informing me the developments taking in the oil field as he had plenty of time to kill and I had plenty of time to miss him.

He was using the two Felker friendship aircrafts which were at his disposal more often than required to refer his patients to city hospital care and the administration was curious about it. But his authority was not sublimed by the desert climate and desert lifestyle. I believe most of the workers were British and locals. One British is the worst enemy of another British, I was given to understand. Somehow his reliever arrived early and he was relieved and he conveyed that he would be returning shortly. He also hated the desert takeoffs and desert landing of small aircraft which would flew with a blur and land with a thud. He had lost his appetite and weight, but I was happy for his return and started preparing for his reception. The day he was expected, I decided to take a tub bath, got up early, filled the tub with Luke-warm water just sufficient not to over spill. I poured the liquid soap and spat and splashed bubbles on the surface. I got in, applied shampoo in excess, scrubbed myself and felt good while the residents, including his friend and kids were still asleep.

I enjoyed the relaxation and spent as much time as I could in the tub, also expecting Doctor's return to step in and join me. The door opened and I closed my eyes pretending to avoid soap water getting into my eyes. I was half immersed in the bubbles and his bachelor friend found me in the tub bare above my waist. He stood bolt uptight and stunned. I was continuing my bathing ritual and he never expected me to rise so early for a bath. The silence made me to open my eyes and our eyes met. In embarrassment I immersed myself completely and he was surprised of my slipping in and became confused. He pulled me out from the immersion, holding my arm pits.

He said, 'You would die this way'. He left bathroom immediately.

I shouted. 'Close the door behind you, please'.

He hid his distorted face and quickly ushered out. I knew it was unintentional incident to be ignored and continued with my cleansing the back with sponge handle. Shortly thereafter I came out wearing my bathrobe and a towel surrounding folded wet hair, wrapped tightly to absorb water before applying hair dryer. I saw his friend stirring his tea longer than required in the kitchen, obviously preoccupied in his thoughts. Soon he moved into his room and I heard the main door closed with an unexpected noise and he left for his duty. Sooner Doctor made his appearance. He himself looked dirt shriveled and I pointed my finger to the bathroom for him to take a quick bath, while I switched on the hair dryer and Doctor came out fresh and clean.

'Were you naked in there'? was his first question.

I wonder how he imagined a situation which took place sometime back. Probably he saw his friend climbing down stairs or riding his car out of parking lot or whatever. His eyes were fixed on my face and his lips expressive of mischief. He stretched his hand and slowly played with a strand of my hair tickling my throat. All safe and accounted for, it took sometime for me absorb the scene of the accidental mishap and in the hind sight I was still looking out of the bedroom unnecessarily, but not caring if his friend sees us to get flattened like a pancake.

'I am good', I said.

The animation on Doctor's face was rained and he jocularly told me,

'You better warn people to knock doors before entering but do thank him for this time'. We embraced each other as though we met after a decade.

We had good time while kids were still asleep and I felt if this show of mutual affection would continue, then I would be dancing the 'fire and earth quake drill'. I saw the intensity of emotions on his face, while he slept and I prepared meals for the unit. Kids were wither overfed or required extra sleep that they were not awakened. Having nothing better to do, I slowly crept beside him and stretched the quilt over our heads. The closeness and warmth were making me feel sleepy, but Doctor was awake probably anticipating this move and we liked foreplay and after play and remained in bed until kids were fully awake and my girl was pulling my feet and started calling to get up for her feed. I looked into the cradle and found my boy also kicking his legs in the air for want of change of diapers. I undertook the liabilities and took a quick shower and waited on the dining table for Doctor to join.

We were in no moods to go out and felt lazy, so remained indoors playing with kids and watching cartoons, entwined on the sofa. I thought of encountering him in this leisure time. I told him about what I witnessed from the key hole, lacking in any punitive tone. He remained in the same leisure posture. It was a right move but at a wrong time.

'See, it was like what took place this morning with you. We are surrounded by sincerely appreciative people, who are deprived of certain necessary provisions against their hormonal surges mostly induced by social inhibitions. And good thing you enquired, otherwise I would have questioned you for your honest sincerity. Rather I was waiting for your call on this issue, which has no bearing in long term relationships. One has to be considerate towards humanity at large and that is mandatory for exchanges of considerations towards one another'. Doctor was good at lectures.

What an explanation he has given me. We were grown up people indulging in reciprocal expressions. It only takes a little effort to magnify as etiquettes. I participated without getting congratulated. Doctor shook his head in a gesture meaning, his loss of getting convinced by such misunderstandings. His gesture was like an ice-cream van in hell. I resigned with a hysterical amnesic profile and recited my frustration in understanding his logic. He made an expensive apologetic expression of resignation which he keeps in reserve out of sheer habit. I didn't want to entertain him with an uncanny smile. He looked into my eyes with insensitivity before grimacing a twisted face.

I sat down in a fluid motion with casual propping of one ankle over the opposite knee. His manner of expression was advisory with insufficiency. His flocks of strands of hair brushed his forehead with the breeze coming from the window. I was not three decades too old for getting so deflated. I quirked my eyebrows at him and his skin color changed to deep crimson. His lips tightened in a thin line. The look on his face was between scorn and amusement. I felt like pasting a few feathers, slap a target ring on my chest and be ready for a shot. It turned out into a hit and very palpable hit, not on him but on me. I missed out my calling as a primary school teacher. I didn't get any perverse pleasure in rendering me as obnoxious as it could become.

I should improvise next time, otherwise I couldn't stand a chance in hell to win over him, while he sat in complete silence. In is books my efforts are entitled recognizably ineffectual and he turned his gaze towards me, half turning and resting his hand over my thigh. His speculation of what his decisions would be in future encounters of any kind would remain a final verdict, immaterial of the pain it may inflict on me or his capacity to handle or absorb surprises. I preferred a pause to agree to get strangulated.

He gave an identical gesture of resignation, so often repeated from his side. A sort of submission to the facts without yielding to its essence value. He gave another curious look of exasperation towards me.

'Men are given a special leeway in the public eye in matters of liberties', he added a denouncement.

My expression was that of undivided attention and total listening attitude. He was showing like a bad boy, who has become a deviant and I wished I could cross line him. It was more like a character assassination to him. I wondered, if my walking out would be considered a mean gesture. I also didn't want to break the persistent understandings between us.

UNAVOIDABLE CONDITIONS

I was returning back to home country after almost a decade. It was planned but you never know the turn arounds. Doctor got a lot of money from gratuity, bonuses and what not. He also carried an airport visa just in case of some surprise. We also brought a lot of electronics and furnishings after shift of residence allowances. The preparation and travel were tedious and tiring. I was fatigued to my last reserve of energy. We were also apprehensive about the custom duty, if encountered by some prejudiced officer. We walked out coolly through 'nothing declarable' green gate. It was a relief but I almost fainted and took Doctor's support to sit back and felt like lying down. The custom officials were curious about the picture. They probably thought we escaped some penalties. We were out from the arrivals lounge and kids followed sticking to my legs. We were home.

There was nobody to receive us. The reception was cold instead of tropical climate. We managed to seek hired help and stuffed the baggage in the taxies and rode separately to reach home. Welcome home. Home country with second largest population in the world. Crowds everywhere, but no acquaintances. All strangers. We were strangers in our own home-land. That I could live with, but what I found testing on my nerves were the noises in the streets of vendors hauling, vehicle engines grumbling on worn out machines, shutters squeaking with loud thunder and people shouting for no reason. There were clusters of vehicles making noises while passing by, buss horns honking and constant chattering of crowds were pulsating in my ears. Tires of two, three or four wheelers screeching, so dysrhythmic, which were echoing in my head and everyone shouting at the top of their voices debating was becoming unbearable.

All were provoking my repentance and hammering on my mind, as though I am a celebrity overestimating my arrival after winning a gold medal in some unknown sports activity of Olympics. I felt if I continue giving importance to this noise pollution, I may myself start labelling me a minor reality show star or a saleable news event, which may appear as headline in next day's newspaper. Doctor's grimness on his face was equally distressing to me. His fingers were iron tight on his briefcase handle and I was sure he may lose his temper soon enough. His feelings about lack of reception added to my fear.

'Keep up your poise, as I will not be surprised if we find the receivers of the arrival lounge still at home, preparing to go to departure lounge instead', he whispered in my ears.

I resisted my urge to pull a face at him. One more irresponsible act from me would set off the episode of a time passing row between us. Actually, it curiously made me to misbehave but I kept my reserve and remained under control. Kids were looking at the crowds with amazement or amusement, I was not sure of. I let fresh air gush in from my side of the window of taxi and I took a deep breath to relax and compose myself. Doctor was right, as we saw families of both sides over crowding our house. They were still there trying to depart to get arrivals. I release my elbow from his forearm where it was resting for some release of tension. I was disappointed by seeing disappointment on faces of my side of the family. My parents seemed dissatisfied with my weight loss after two successive deliveries and follow up fitness exercises. It was the first eyeroll from my father to welcome home. He was not the type to appreciate it, in spite of the healthy profile I generated as my presence. The voices in the house were replaced by cries of recognition, funny giggles and small talk among adult males. I came from a country where the only noises come from birds chirping in the mornings and sea waves tiding with soothing calmness at the sea shores in the evening.

Every one was shouting to be heard and it was the occupational hazard of under developed countries trying to get recognition of a developed civilized country. Everyone seemed to shout for their livelihood. My irritation was growing with passing time. Doctor's shoulder was leaning a little on me for his stability. He would probably question the absence of reception at the airport. I was apprehending that I may not tempt him to question as he will not get any sensible answer. No body even bothered to explain to him the reasons, even if they care to apologize or give an hour's delay in arrival schedule which was spread as a rumor. I never expected anyone to spell forgiveness about their messed up starting time.

Doctor remained quiet and I smiled in appreciation of his tolerance threshold. It was a calculated but manufactured gesture of appreciation. My dimples appeared on my cheeks and Doctor appeared to have come under control. Everything came under control also because I tied a pony tail instead of beads on my hair. Everyone got busy in shifting luggage while we rested in unclean sofa seating of our drawing room, which seem needed a thorough cleaning. Mothers-in law kept looking and drifting between all of us. I was fond of the older one and the younger was kind but reserved. Doctor's brother lived next door and his restless kids were also overwhelmingly noisy. This family would be our neighbors for long, was my guess. His brother's wife was chattering with nobody in particular. His brother came with his hands thrust into his pant pockets, made quick enquiries of welfare and left.

I had to announce, more for the benefit of all including us that the cargo will arrive in a couple of weeks' time. The crowd started moving one after the other, as though they were waiting for us to unpack the luggage and pass on their gifts.

'You take some rest'. I addressed to Doctor but all others to hear.

I was myself feeling a bit unsteady on my feet. The crowd liquidated in no time from optimism to pessimism and may return in a couple of weeks. Mothers-in-law were living upstairs and we were to occupy downstairs was the arrangement made prior to our arrival. The kitchen was downstairs and would remain under my supervision. The old ladies had two bedrooms one for each, a separate toilet and bath facility, a hall to watch TV and entertain their guests and a balcony to sit and pass time. They should be happy with this arrangement.

My personality didn't alter a bit even under strange tropical atmosphere or out side influence. Doctor was genuinely appalled and looked at me with gratitude for this announcement. He knew there is difference between brushing off stress and having clear ideas of problem solving. I would continue to use my abilities and potential. I also didn't feel any sisterly or related feeling for our neighbor lady and it must be the same with Doctor, in spite of she being his brother's wife. She also became defensive and retreated to her premises. I maintained my effort to let the house get vacated completely. Old ladies slowly climbed up and servants went to their quarters and we took a sigh of relief. I was getting wisdom and learning to survive. I understood one has to keep distances near or far to level with your comfort zone. I managed to feed the kids and Doctor helped himself and we slept.

Next day morning I saw a stylish suited man at the front gate looking for call bell. He found it and pushed to hear a ring while I opened the door to enquire as to how I could be of any help. He was looking for another house. My hunched shoulder didn't go along with my bored expression. Any body can push the bell and disturb for nothing. It is customary to disturb people for petty directions or silly answers. Doctor was up wiping his face with impatience, as he was to join his work or to give joining report.

Instead he went to directorate and applied for extension of joining time and he was called in immediately into the ante-room. NRIs are always preferred in the home country. Doctor I believe passed on the Champaign bottle brought with a brand which was director's favorite and he came back. The director was obliged to favor him for already exchanged considerations and he must have remembered it well, because he gave six months of extension to join his service. He was half expecting it and so, there was no need to get excited about.

The difference was in spite of a secured government job offer, it had to start with a contract service before regularization, all the benefits to be enjoyed later. It was the initial time which warranted adjustments. I was ready for it but not him. He was still weighing the pros and cons. But at least it allowed a time span to think and rethink and plan. Doctor also wanted to revisit north Africa to settle some unfinished scores. Good that he had contacts here and there which always come handy in times of need. As to what may truly happen was unpredictable. The plus and minus points were obvious but the suitability of time was of prime importance. Moreover, the changing political scenario around the world also needed to be revised. I was not sure when things would fall into proper places.

During this time, we moved around leaving children with their grandmothers, which was an advantage. We looked around for additional landed properties, gave our already purchased apartments for rental value and Doctor's mothers also wanted division of assets well in advance, while they were in good health. They had crossed their ages to remain in good health and that was an additional concern which bothered him. He also had to put the kids to proper schools. The trend was of branded school's admissions to be achieved as a status symbol. The cargo was received and gadgets implanted inside. The refrigerator was outsized for the dining area. The washing machine suited the bathroom corner and additional hired help procured for easy living.

The traffic on roads was a menace, taking time and exertion for locomotion. Doctor also had to self-introduce himself to the local area private hospitals for association and possible private practice. I stopped nursing my boy and started monthly periods. He didn't want me to be subjected for yet another caesarean section, fourth could be tormenter and we volunteered from our ends, he for vasectomy and me for tubectomy. His friend lady gynecologist suggested to postpone until his return from north Africa. We had already shifted in favor of other contraceptive methods. Life was definitely not as convenient as we were used to it.

The plan was set, he left us in custody of his mothers and went. I had by then learned some facts about missing periods indicative of conception and I became pregnant again in his absence. Ignorance becomes a blessing in disguise. I could not count the number of weeks but I knew, I would set in labor after his arrival. He was informed about this development. He remained silent away from home. His silence left me blushed and breathless. I could imagine an edge of temper on his forehead. I was almost biting my nails. I felt he wanted to assure me. There were no doubts circumventing our relationship. The child was his and he had to decide it himself. I dreamt his mischievous smile and I kicked him playfully at his shin. He seemed to vocalize, about his leg getting hurt and I amused him by saying that I am sure it is not broken. Sanity returned and I woke up.

He returned earlier than my expected date of delivery, but not before our auto-rikshaw somersaulted while we were returning from industrial exhibition held once every year, pedestrians pulled us out and we could hold our weights on our feet, but no harm done. I was subjected to fourth LSCS and a look alike of Doctor, baby girl was born. The surgeon removed my uterus and the chapter of child bearing was closed for ever, as per destined fates. Three children were a happy family unit and we were contented with what was blessed. He joined his place of work in old city as we lived in new city. The distance of every day travel was long and arduous, especially in adverse weather conditions with growing blockade of traffic. Life must be hard for Doctor to get acclimatized with new weather conditions, new colleagues, new premises, new patients, new working methods and everything new.

He was also working on getting his private practice established in the evening like other Doctors. We needed extra funds for our growing family and growing demands. All this was a stern blow on the civility of a man who if given option would have preferred farming in the country side. He used to return tired and exhausted, would take a short afternoon nap and get out to attends calls from surrounding hospitals, making several ins and outs per day. Kids were happy having found additional pair of hand for their needs and new friends made in the locality. I discarded all irrelevant worries and assisted him in his needs and wants. But I also noticed a change in him and not towards better.

We couldn't find leisure hours to discuss the provisions and comparisons of struggles. His old-time friends and their families started visiting us. His patients at times visited our place with gratitude and gratefulness of Doctor's cures. But from the perspective of broken relationships he had discarded all his previous affairs, like stray socks. He would casually introduce me to his new-found contacts both gents and ladies and I would vibrate with despair. Doctor was not the same person anymore, as though he had turned into default settings. He would always drop any pretense of indifference towards his old or new contacts. He has changed into a spoiled brat, but he was wise enough to avoid showing off any resentment towards me. He has always conquered over me like a knight putting his sword and seem ready for other measures.

The neighbors in spite of being relatives and that too closed ones, had been a source of constant harassment to us. Their children growing up faster than usual were teasing and torturing our kids. They would increase their infiltration more when Doctor is away from home. But I was blessed by his friend's arrival especially when he was not around, who was a decent person and plain, simple helpful man. He would keep me company and will exchange small talk and pass my time and advise me to remain calm and composed, immaterial of neighbor's taunts and tricks and gimmicks which they got accustomed to enact and enjoy. My mother-in-law's shouts and yelling used to shrink me and frighten me. I was not used to such things at my home, with my side of family of parents and relatives. There were inhibitions and restrictions done without shouting or yelling. I was also obliged to serve the old ladies, which I used to do by serving their meals even if they are asleep so that they don't complain of having left hungry.

TIME-BOUNDED TIMES

I thought I will let go of everything, my life, Doctor's life, children's lives and mothers-in law and their indifference. Their bossing around, their untimely demands their unreasonable requests, people's philosophical criticism and all kinds of poetic elongations of my rivals and my solitude, their timely advances and people's open flirting with me. I get incredible dreams about Doctor having four wives, as justified by faith under mis-conceptual understanding and me included and his spending time judiciously with all together at one time. His claims of justice done on religious grounds and my subsequent suffering. I dream of being reborn with wings and flapping them to go around the world. I dream of lightening falling on a tree under which I was taking temporary shelter.

I dream about my parents coming back expecting me to do post-graduation in domestic violence, I dream of me as an old-time heroine singing songs circling bushes. I dream and dream during my REM sleep to get up in Non-REM sleep forgetting them all, with no recollections. No amount of concentration could bring them back to the surface of my memory. Nobody would like to dream and forget as I do. People want to dream of becoming queen of Victorian times or bandit queen of mountain ranges, they also wish to dream about pre-historic robust idols to be worshiped by fools, who have made them themselves. All stupidity which is intolerable. I can't tolerate such dreams. Dreams can't come to me on time bound basis, they should be random and discrete and not worth remembering. But the blinding facts were constantly cheated and robbed and stolen of our amenities. The neighbors were seeking for chances to exploit, taunt and ridicule me or even acting mean without reason. They would always provoke our tranquility by lifting useful things and I would worry searching them here and there.

I don't want surprises, but unconsciously I give surprises to others. I get surprised so often and I like surprises occasionally, more so with Doctor, but not so much with kids. I want people to congratulate me for having transformed from a domesticated girl to a woman of substance. I want to do jogging in snow with ear phones plugged into my ears, listening to folk music. I wonder whether I would be able to do pilgrimage on my own, when at some time in the past I had difficulty riding a bus to fancy market. I want to be encouraged to prepare royal delicacies even if they are unpalatable or get burnt a little in the bottom. I assume everybody will be fine without me and I am fine without anybody else, except Doctor. That will be a good solution to my intolerance to stupidity or tolerance to wisdom.

I would stop thinking about tomorrow, as tomorrow never comes. I will live in today and not in yesterday. Just today at this moment only. It will be better than any other time, only if Doctor is with me. He is a passionate man and I see passion in eyes to eyes contact. He is a sensitive person, but not as much as I am. I punctuated myself to ignore people's mistakes. I forgive people and forget them. I give several chances to others to prove themselves. I don't know whether I am stupid or genius. Not for me but for youngsters to try out, for being able to manage new dresses in new found land's opportunities. I want appraisal and should get applauded for my ability to keep my in-laws in good books, my smiles which are mistaken as invitations, my untiring energy to serve the family, my simplicity which can be easily exploited, my well keeping a relationship of abuse with Doctor who could play tricks and games and could get away unperturbed, my impulsive decision and influence to migrate in between continents, my inbuilt intrinsic dimple which is a source of appeal and my handling of abuse like a cat and mouse chase.

I wonder how we were brought in wedlock with diverse types of species we were, what sort of contrast we were lodging in ourselves. I know marriages are made in heaven and this combination was destined. Mortals had no control over sickness and health birth and death, the rest is given under our control by God to exercise judgement for our own good or bad. We can set up alarms to get up early or allow us to sleep till afternoon, take tea or soda and then stroll in parks or while away time in gossip till late evening and watch TV till might to repeat the routine or the next day. I found it gross but fascinatingly gross that I can control my urges and Doctor cannot. My kids are no matter what they do are sincere towards their responsibilities. They are into brands, where as I don't.

Me and Doctor had lived together for quite long but we remained apart. We were never the same, we were different. I loved folk songs and he liked old melodies, I loved family dramas and he liked documentaries, I read and he writes. I eat cooked non-veg food and he eat raw vegetables. I wish to leave a low profile and he wants to be on top. What a difference of personalities to have lasted for so long. I prefer leisure and wants to remain busy. I have no worry to pass time and he finds means of killing time. I am melancholic and he is manic. I love something else and he likes something else. I am free with my children and he remain reserved with them. With so many differences and so long a sustained relationship, either I had been stupid or he is stupid. I had a lot of tolerance and he had no tolerance or we both didn't. I didn't want to know.

There was no need of knowing what I had not known for so long. I can't start dating him. I don't want to sleep in a different room and he in another room. I go to him for questions and he come to me for answers. I didn't want to exchange slips of papers with messages in each other's absence and still get along fine. I didn't want to be separated with partitions or curtains and still remain friends. What an interesting relation to survive with. I always wanted to be with my children and he preferred to remain at a distance with them. I wanted to celebrate birth days and he wanted to mourn on them. I enjoyed attending weddings and he likes to go to funerals. I don't want to wait until internet revolution crops up and he was happy with replacement of computers with type writers. I wished to have smart phones and he was contended with land lines. All this is a big difference.

Later along with passing time things also started changing. Plans kept changing, programs kept changing and we kept changing with the changing times. The endangered species also changed from fishes to crocodiles, from wood peckers to penguins, from whales to dolphins, from roses to lilies. Words became important than languages and meanings became important than contents. Sentences fall out from mouth and die at our feet, vocabulary became important than grammar. I felt like joining school again for further learning. I had been poor in math and good in embroidery. I was good at speaking and poor in listening, again yet another contrast between me and Doctor. He was a good listener from whispers to songs, from screams of patients in pain to calmness of those relieved of pain. I believed that those who have leisure are successful and he thought paucity of time is a measure of success.

I wasn't able to sleep well these days. How pathetic of me to have reached this age and to feel the need of some initiation. Someone told me that excess of contrast become matches. I didn't want to be very rich and very famous. What will people do by becoming successful. It is crazy to think about name and fame also. I didn't want to be an honest civil servant all my life to retire with meagre pension. It is not sane thinking. But I have not failed in my life after living with Doctor and been subjected to four surgeries for three children. It is stupid of me to feel that I have failed and failed to satisfy people. It was as if I was hit at my face by a loser. It shouldn't matter to me if I am outcasted from my father's property. I didn't want material assets, as I had in plenty by the grace of God.

Doctor's mother gave my daughter an antique of silverware, a sieve upon which the neighbors came launching attack on us and fought and fought with me and his mother. They always taught their children that Doctor is filthy rich and they should be 'Robin Hoods' and take away their undeserved shared from us. They always demanded for some or the other from us and used to feel good about it. On festivals the exchanges were unequal but necessary. I was asked to cook delicacies for them and they would ignore us even to invite, when their turn comes. They were partial and squeezing types and sadistic in getting pleasure out of harming us. Their attitudes were menacing and hurtful. Doctor would ask me to ignore but it is easily said than done. The times of economic adjustment warranted him to do extra duties for extra payments and I used to suffer the domestic violence from in-laws for no mistake of mine.

It wasn't academic thinking that I have not achieved anything in life. It is a tattoo. A windfall will change achievements. When I had a great life, why I should feel competitive for nothing. Doctor started from square one and acquired academic excellence, money comes and goes. He helped people, people who needed help. I was at one time a baby and a girl asking for favors. Now I am not obliged to ask for favors from people. Doctor also think it is absurd to seek favors lightly to be rejected lightly. He also kept saying that it is always good to be vegetarian, as you have lesser options like lesser evils. I didn't have any specific choices or options. I didn't want to be a part of organizing team of conferences, even though I enjoyed them. I need not be what people expect me to be.

I had healthy children, physical well being provided by me and mental well-being given by Doctor. It was all awesome. I was grateful to God for having given more than what I deserved. Actually, I deserved nothing, as though I am discarded by a business in a trip for which I was willing to pay. Travel is travel in any class and it would remain a stress immaterial of who is involved or distances to be travelled. Travel a temporary journey to end somewhere, let it be any destination. What is the big deal to get timebound luxuries to return back to normalcy. There shouldn't be downfall from normalcy. I would remain excited with economy class in travel. Maybe others may not agree with me. They have different choices and different options to select. All options get old fashioned in the end. All those exotic destinations fade away with time. It is the manifestation of contentment which remains till the end and matters too.

Why should I drift into olden days, I love the present world and the world loves me reciprocally? I didn't go wrong and I don't have to believe in idealism. I had talent and contact, enough for satiety in life. Reliance on talent is good or bad, I don't know and I don't care. If I can't play or compose melodies it is not my fault. If I get hungry I should get food. I don't have to be very ambitious. What do ambitious people get except some medals, some grants, some trophies. They get nothing. It doesn't do any good. I need not encounter anybody for those ideals. There will be ups and downs, deviations and straight paths, obstacles and freeways, profits and losses, failures and achievements, and so on. I think I am confident but I am not, Doctor thinks he is a genius but he is not. Having great ambitions, great plans, great programs or great ideas, so what. All get such impressions but that doesn't mean they are crazy. No, it means they are cool, as long as they remain cool.

If one gets pride then he is a loser. If one has regrets he is loser again. I don't have to nurture regrets as regrets doesn't help. It becomes so pretentious and I am not a robber, or a mobster or a thief to live on other's credits. It will be foolish on my part to think like that. I don't want all those great ideas or plans. What is coherent is how time is being spent. Doctor claims all this is absurd. It is his outlook. Everything he thinks is from below upwards or from above downwards or like jigsaw puzzle. What if he couldn't go to Harvard, Oxford or Cambridge or AIMS. He will remain as much as his IQ will allows. He is qualified to prescribe, whether he is prescribing right medication to wrong people or vice versa. He has lot of decisions to make and he is doing it and he will continue doing the same.

I sometimes lose the essence of time in my aimless wander. I can even lose my accommodation. I should do things which all others are doing and I am not unhappy about it. I don't want to switch around, rather I should avoid competing with others. We are all underdogs doing something for impact, cool or un-cool. So, what. I can miss out on certain things, like first choices can be missed, first chances can be missed, first attendance can be missed, first reward can be missed, first crush can be missed, and so on and I should not think in excess. I should remain cool and compact like great people of history. They were all second-class students, I may be third class to start with and end up becoming second class.

I always tell Doctor that he is right, not because he is always right but because he resents having been told wrong. I am different and he is different.

I watch TV serials full of dramas with jealousy and hatred, he watches calm and soothing aerial views of resorts. There is nothing wrong with me and there is nothing wrong with him. But there is something grossly wrong with us. I want to donate and he wants to seek donations. He says seeking donations makes a person humble. He prefers to clothe simple coverings and I want to camouflage myself with decorations to look good and attractive. Not to others but to my own reflections of myself in mirror. He wants to appear plain and simple and I want to appear gorgeous and flamboyant. I want to talk about everybody and he doesn't talk about others. I like ceremonies and he doesn't. I like get togethers and he likes solitude.

I wonder how we exchanged so much of give and take between us. How much of fun we shared. We always remained on the opposite sides of the fence at any given time, except in matters of conjoint interest we both come on one side only. It creeps me out when I count the number of friends he has or had and it creeps me out as how he could sustain relationship with all, especially when he is not forgetful even if he forgives. Hs feeling toward me was mutual most of the time, but there are exceptions to rule. In general people should bother about their problems and not others. Doctor bothers about nothing, not even my opinions. Either he is smart of he is a moron.

PLEASING DISPLEASURES

Doctor still had to prove himself, contribute to the non-disclosures of words and justifications with the actual happenings which were still unconvincing. No doubt they are not worth committing to my memories and in the end better to be forgotten and in future and to refrain from redoing, conditioned as good riddance. I was obliged to bear the repercussions of his formed opinions and dictating terms, but I cannot reject them as spam or trash or junk to be deleted for good. He has to have faith in me and the virtues of our religion, anybody inclusive to be proud of, down the road. That is the ground reality of living a relationship with gainful results.

One night, Doctor demanded or rather requested something and I denied. He was not expecting it and he went to the drawing room and lied down on the sofa. I couldn't make it a regular habit and realized I should allow the rehearsal of past drill, not fire or earth quake type this time. I had to go to him breathe on his face to make him aware that it is imperfection in the arena of marital relationships to sleep on the sofa. It became inevitable for me to do the challenge properly and I did and I could drag him out, back to bed. I expected an explosion of charged emotions, which didn't take place. I also didn't want his hand to remain tightly entwined with fingers, prominently displaying his confusion. I also didn't want to strip his ego to abject apology. I decided then and there that Doctor's deviant requests or demand made only occasionally shouldn't be declined again.

I practically collapsed on bed obviously exhausted and he flecked an invisible speck from my shoulder and I seemed to have taken control of the situation without twitching my eyelids. We descended to a routine repetition of the drama which took place sometime back, appeared an ambiguity. It was a reflection of human guilt over a poorly written screen play. I taunted at him about his sleeping on sofa and he smiled broadmindedly. It was yet another expression of intense righteousness. I wished I should have known better and life returned to where it started. Doctor only raised his eyebrows and neither of us were ready for another ploy of fake argument. It seemed a waste of time, as we both were fulfilled with appraisal for each other's care. In spite of me being admittingly little bitter, the learnings were of great help in the end.

He should consider opinions of loved ones, not just depending on his self-righteous formed opinions. He needed guidance from God. God, Oh God, guide him to be considerate towards me, if not for me let it be for his own formed opinions of righteousness at least. His formed opinions had given him nothing at times. A realization should get dawn on him sooner or later. He was weird person and a messed-up guy. He is sensitive to the extent of pollen allergy and he feels bad if not invited. But he would say even if invited he wouldn't have gone. He has inflated ego boundaries. He is mostly available in times of my needs and occasionally not when I needed him most. He says needs should be need based and modest but not affluent. He believes in piety and religiosity but he lacks in both. He started writing books but could not edit them. He commits mistakes but is unwilling to admit them. I think he is suffering from giddiness and cannot overcome it.

He thinks he has great thinking standards when I doubt he is, he is empty headed. Better still hollow from inside. He is always desperate to claim victories, as though he is Prince charming, but he is good looking and may look even better in the column of obituaries. He envies all others for having successfully fooled around with others. How does it matter now? People have their own lives to live the way they want. I think he should listen to old melodies and remain satisfied by doing nothing. He spares questions to himself first, but when he doesn't come up with sensible answers he makes other people to pay for his inabilities. He is an abusive type, a scumbag to be brief. He is orchestrated to be a nut-head in a nut shell.

I used the term loosely and complimented on my appetite, dieting, exercise to shape my curves and contours, in spite of a cunning web of lines indicating previous pregnancies. I felt like tying a pony tail to my daughter and another on myself. I imagined my reflection in the mirror stooping low and felt sourness. It looked like I have stumbled on my syllables and forgotten punctuations. It had even driven me to thoughts of self-mutilations briefly. I was not wearing that beige color dress, as I saw Doctor's reflection in the background and I heard a remark in appreciation and I gave him an elbow jostle. My mind instantly went into a state pf panic on remembrance of that incidence. I should focus on the bottom lines. I better be in bed with a vanilla ice-cream cone melting and dribbling on my fingers.

At that moment I felt as though I am an over-worked clerk tired of the burden of files she has to go through and sent it to authorities for signatures. Doctor's convincingly fake smile was found pasted on his lips. He was wearing an incorrectly buttoned shirt as usual, asking me to re-button it in an orderly fashion. I blinked at the imagination of the picture on the beach shot by somebody from a bad angle showing the beige dress clinging to my skin and amalgamating in flesh color. It made me feel like an offering for sacrifice. It maybe stimulating to some but it was irritating to my eyes. I glanced at him like a cat and mouse chase, but his lips were tightened like the fold of a purse zipped completely. It was not going for publication to be seen on central spread of a magazine for adults.

I cannot kill a bird even if a shooting and hunting sets all packed in my handbag. I grumbled to myself. I should leave everything and become a historian. Historical opinions differ about preaching places. Debates undertaken denoted the suspicion whether they were annexures to group meeting of ministers earlier or to group cat walks of models in between. I brushed all these ideas aside. Doctor was still standing by my side inspecting my body, as though he is a celebrated detective to find some clue out it. I thought of asking him, if he had long term friends why he prefers to remain aloof until called upon. He intentionally loose them to brood later. Good thing he doesn't believe in non-profit organization self-declarations, while making good profits or the out-sourcing system and its mythology of circuitous lies of well organized profit-making business.

I decided not to throw any temper tantrums, neither would ask Doctor to pay for the damages I could claim. It could do only as much harm as expected out of disposable plates. To other women it may go un-noticed but to me it was a preplanned covert operation to shook the harmony of our relationship. I flinched for his sake and his smile was ready to be offered for chewing. I was sure he wouldn't enlarge and plant it in our drawing room wall. But one cannot be very sure of what Doctor thinks and what he does later. I swallowed on my dry mouth but any publicity is good publicity. I would make everyone's life a complete chaos until my mood improves. Doctor's gaze was curious and apprehensive, there was a bit of impatience in his attitude, a rare condition to be seen. I was not meant for sarcasm, scrutiny or entertainment.

I was on the verge of agitation reaching to violent tendencies. I may not mind if I manifest a hate crime or become a scandal for nothing. It is socially un-acceptable and I wanted my grievance to be heard, even if I am trying to convert a flop show into a successful story by giving free tickets to fill the chairs. I cannot miss the implications and this was a final word. Moreover, I was a publicist to exhibit like a shriveled balloon subjected to a worst pop. I was wavering between speculation and reluctant fascination and avoiding to utter accusing remarks. I some how managed to find my voice to restart. Nothing came out of nothing as nothing existed. My voice started rising in pitch and my tone resounding annoyance. I recalled how I failed to notice in a meeting, how Doctor's cuff-links caught on my dress, while I was getting up and it tore beyond expected limits. It was my favorite and expensive dress. I couldn't care less for my bare thigh. I was repenting at the loss of a likable item.

I had plenty in my wardrobe marginally placed without a sequence, among the purchases of common market street bargains. But my cheeks were getting pinker and warmer out of embarrassment of having been exposed in public. I moved laterally to hide, but certain tears are literal tears. I became self-conscious of my image but the thought of jumping to bed with Doctor would not sublime the image. I felt like a hebephrenic but it was not a stereotyped action which could warrant an explanation, neither an applaud from the spectators. I was not trying to seek public sympathies and people expect me to move on, even if I was trading off. Doctor gave an apologetic look and a placatory smile, which I found not endearing. I wished to push myself to walkout as if nothing had happened.

It was unethical, but ethics are reserved for businesses and not for me. It seemed like a resounding implication of my story of an unfair dismissal to the media and I am a movie star even if that is of a 'B' grade flop. Without rendering a full value and showing hasty mannerisms to repent thereafter, another person attempted to boss around with me, by his boasting nature productive of grandiosity. He communicated his street smartness by certain misguidance and later got caught. One more self-proclaimed man, claiming Doctorate in ethics of human sciences, actually harmed by his own confused mindset asked some favors from me which I could not grant. All small-timers, embezzlers and retards, whose bodies outgrown their minds, also were skeptical of my nature and appearance and tried to defame me but they were not even worth dime a dozen and didn't deserve a second thought.

All these experiences worth recording were lessons for their progeny to improvise in future and they were not strangers to me. Unfortunately, they were related with us and relationships for formality sake also had to be covered. One couldn't resist his promiscuity and nail a girl of different faith which could have been politicized if not for Doctor's intervention. Another one attempted day light robbery, forged signature and withdrew money from the bank and interrogation pointing to his finger printing made him to confess and he was also forgiven. Yet another one when introduced to a celebrity exploited the contact and maneuvered treachery but forgotten. There was one more bow-legged dwarf of a man consolidated as a friend attempted to cheat us and almost succeeded until he got paranoid and started hiding himself.

I remember my feelings when his insane idealism which he considered as his sense of purpose sloped and gushed into dust. Colonialism has gone into dust in history. Doctor didn't believe in private schools because he was a product of public school and he became a complete productive jewel for no reason and became acceptable in society. He was imaginative with negative thinking except for his pseudo-philosophical ideologies. I felt he better learn now. Better late than never, instead of being early for an un-appointed interview for that matter.

He was insomniac but he would disagree with the diagnosis. He would secretly swallow tranquilizers and I wanted him to shift to anti-depressants. He honestly wanted to make an impact in the world, without introducing himself and he would get preoccupied in out dated theories, which used to get vanished in thin air in no time. I wanted to summarize his personality and wanted to make him understand that he had made mistakes and is still making even in his career, but he would refuse admitting. He was a sold-out product, which didn't have an integrity in it. He was struggling but he would disconnect himself with the fact. He was just lucky that he had not been a prey to his predators.

Doctor hated male privileges, white privileges and racial discrimination but he was a racist himself. A proud intellectual with no intelligence. He had enough to remain thankful without admitting it. What was wrong in admitting mistakes. People learn by mistakes more than achievements. He would hold long boring meetings within family and I couldn't stop thinking about the contempt he used to feel good out of it. I was sure in spite of hating luxury, if he gets one taste of it he would be better. He was a serial in himself with episodes to lengthen the drama. What all was given was give out of mercy from God. He was awesome in few things and awful in others, others out numbering the few. He got what he didn't expect and he expected what he didn't get. It was a demonetized judgement with a wrongly passed verdict.

INHIBITED BOUNDARIES

People collaborated with their fantasies to falsify the facts and performed treachery with us and betrayal of our trust in them, demanding explanations, so I should not try finding who is unethical or who is not. They compelled us for lineage, disrupted our tranquility and continued with their furtive conduct and preposterous conversation, which was very derogatory and false explanatory when time came. Just for Doctor's information I declared that no sensible person will encourage relations to such treacherous and unreasonable people like them. They never bounded themselves by the natural principle of 'honesty' in human relationships and kept narrating half-truths and whole lies, which are now becoming evident by their presumptuous narrow-mindedness that 'businesses are not inherited' the way they inherited and, in all fairness, I should have followed up, unless I planned it to cheat us well in advance and acted untruthfully to successfully fool around with us.

Their own people have pointed out that since long their misdeeds and unlawful acts of covert conspiracy were done without remorse and guilt, and now they are applauding themselves and thinking grandiose by sitting tight with any guiltless customer's money and feeling safe, no doubt having played this game very well but they should be rest assured that there is another court high up to judge and sentence verdicts. Their intentional blames and irrefutable claims were baseless, disgraceful and surreptitious distortions of facts as questionable acts, hence I had to leave things from here to elders and then on to God, almighty and do not bother to reply, as it will not serve any good and lastly discern that problems of any kind bud up around 3 issues, and i.e. via poor tolerance threshold, high expectancy level and rigidity in personality.

There were few characters who had played a role of collateral indifference towards my feelings. They always planned for their selfish motivations to get any chance in sucking out on others. They were morons by birth, morons by upbringing and morons by training. To add to the list of evil doers some were devils in themselves, being products of broken home atmosphere and always blaming others for their faults. They always point fingers at others and were actually paupers more than beggars. Without a logical reason except claiming to be molested as children, justifying their pervert natures were actually fooling around with themselves more than others. I couldn't have helped them and I didn't want to. They were 'have nots' with wishful thinking to become 'haves', given the chance of manifesting extreme mental cruelty on me and abused me for their own uses. They would be questioned for their misdeeds on 'Dooms day' of next life and I didn't want to question them in this life.

They were living in a bubble and dare to look back in their lives of dark past and boast like white day break light of the present. They are actually exhibiting pride, when no where pride is advocated as a righteous act. Pride is not approved by the almighty creator or provider. They would always remain on the edge. They would call other without leaving a voice mail and when they get call-backs they avoid answering. They are lunatics and had to live with it. On the contrary Doctor had his own good righteous side and some godforsaken good qualities. He loved his children, his mothers, me and himself, but while expressing it he would behave as though he is undergoing a surgery warranting amputations. He would keep me posted with all raw facts, details hidden behind thick curtains, which were opaque.

At times my frustration used to get piled up and drained on my kids. They used to get confused upon illogical and unreasonable scolding which they didn't deserve but bore with me. The visits to my parent's house were restricted and I used to get annoyed for this rigorous imprisonment, which did not get any rewards, leave alone any awards. I used to get irritated at the recollection of our times when we used to visit home country from north Africa and were forced to get accommodated in the neighboring apartments to spend nights and to while away days with my in-laws, when Doctor would return early and I used to join him later. Otherwise I was a favorite of all, other extended relatives, new found acquaintances and locality inmates. Everybody used to get useful tips and free medical examinations and treatment out of samples which Doctor always had in spare for the needy. The cousin sister who was desirous to get married to Doctor, had her parents who also cared and solicited their kindness on me.

Doctor was a dreamer and would insist on hearing the bad news first than to bother about the trivialities of good news, even if there is scarcity of good news. He would want his children to touch sky's limits but he would never appreciate their hard work and would keep a critical eye over them. He would be happy helping his family but would never agree to it. He believed in reservations and grace times but would not make any, ignoring them and would remain ready to complain. He was a complete jerk. He would pretend to be regular but he was an absentee. He would cut and crack jokes never heard before and he would narrate incidents which had never happened. He would invent stories after stories and was good at entertaining people. He would pass on message as though verbalizing poetry and keep his secrets to himself. He was a mentor to himself, a self-made man to be honored in his own opinion.

His so called narrow broadmindedness has created these allowances for abusers, which could abuse us. These are happenings in his books and he would wait for the next happening. He was a scared man in spite of being a pillar to the community. He would become defensive on criticism but would claim that criticism is healthy. He even said the best critics are the best friends, but this is humbug and his over valued ideas. He is ready for challenges of any kind without holding any capacity. He would tire himself doing nothing and would not hesitate to self-prescribe medication which he used to prescribe to his patients. What a funny cartoon character he is? He doesn't like competition but if given chance be would beat it to sit behind a large oak paneled desk doing some executive job. From outside he is cool but from inside he is in turmoil.

Things had never been stable with him. He was always undergoing ups and downs.

Doctor was a difficult person to live with. He was not even a friend to himself. He was not genuine and he was twisted. I sometimes think I should call police and hand him over to them. He deserved nothing better than what he is getting from God. He should remain thankful and grateful to his master for being so lenient towards him. He should stop complaining and stop bringing compelling conditions on me, which is a kind of abuse. He is an emotional person, ready for tragedies and would blink back his tears to appear bursting out with laughter aloud. He gets sudden rush of feelings to pop up and tear himself down. He never felt life inside him and never enjoyed my beauty or nature's beauty. He waived off all compliments for me and never remarked any praiseworthy word for me. But his help was unseen and it continued. He would never show off how he is managing but he does.

He tries hard to remain occupied and believed in the phrase that successful people would not know how time passes by. But he had plenty of time to brood. I think he was a nervous wreck about to face a breakdown. He gets doubts about his failures but doesn't think about his achievements. He was full of anguish, grievance and hatred. Even hated himself at times. Only God can give him some solace, some peace of mind, some gift of contentment sounding as free. He whole heartedly accepts the inevitable death but wants it to be sudden and quick. God may put some sense in him. Only then I would get some peace. My peace broken into pieces by his intolerance to stupidity, what a stupid man he is. While I was taking good care of Doctor's mothers I couldn't get any prize instead criticized for some lack of something, which I couldn't help. His mothers never were happy with servant maids, and I would go upstairs and clean their rooms and bath room but they would find some dirt or dust left over which was not tolerated by them. The younger lady was obsessed about cleanliness.

Doctor was a lovable man, he was wise too. I loved him with his limitations, his sarcasms, his seriousness, his laughter to hide his crying, his crying to hide his joy. He is nosy but kind, nasty but understandable, he is crazy but sane. His interpretations of his likable poetry was even better than the poet's interpretation and he had the talent to fabricate evidence of any definition of his own out of anything. I hated to recall the times when I became pregnant in Doctor's absence mis-calculated the missed periods and was suspected foul play by his brother's wife and she would openly talk about my non-existent affairs to defame me. A time came that I started lifting heavy weights and started doing odd things in urgency anticipating a threatened abortion, but fate was written with a different plan and I had to continue with my full term.

Doctor's friends used to take me to reputed obstetricians of the city but his brother's wife was bent upon favoring her own relative to be my care taker during labor and ultimately succeeded in getting things done her way. She forced me to follow up with that surgeon who used to conduct deliveries and used to carry me to his clinic, above which his family used to reside and she would leave me with nurses and would climb upstairs and watch movies and enjoy the company and I was deprived of my rights in many ways. I remember how I fainted in the kitchen and got diagnosed to be pregnant by my mother-in-law and suffered malnutrition and vitamin deficiencies. The adjustment difficulties were paramount in Doctor's absence and I was taxed by the unending strains on my health. I developed blood pressure and was not attended by anyone. On the contrary the multitude of tasks and obligatory shares on my kids were causing them to be deprived of their rights as well.

Once on some impulse I took my kids and left home to my parent's house which was considered a sin next to crime and his brother and sister-in-law made a big fuss and scene out of it and Doctor also transiently didn't approve of my impulsive behavior and I faced severe punitive actions based on one silly mistake. His mothers used to go to treasury office to collect their pensions and made picnics out of those visits and my kids were left drifting for their needs. The neighbor's kids were ready to cause havoc at our place rather than their own and all these notorieties led the Doctor to erect partitions to separate the two units to become different houses and I took a sigh of relief. My younger brother was of big help while he would bypass our house and visit us to attend to petty errands and play with kids. But he was also a teenager then and kid himself. I was not sure why I always hesitated to ask money from the elders and Doctor never allocated any separate pocket money for small requirement of things to get from passing vendors. In short life was hell in his absence.

It was industrial exhibition time, which used to be fun for us. We used to enter through the club, Doctor's friend being the secretary and we could avoid rush and tickets. Once I was given very less time to get ready and I forgot to keep my jewelry bag back into house locker and casually carried it with me. That day there was some celebration and we preferred to ride on a hired Auto-rickshaw. Absentmindedly I kept the heavy jewelry bag in the back space behind the seats and totally forgot to lift it while we reached and were getting down. I paid a tip to the driver, who seemed a nice man and was patient in attitude and careful in driving. Amidst the stalls I recollected suddenly that I had forgotten about the jewelry and went into a shock. I was afraid we had incurred a big loss out of my carelessness. That though kept haunting me until we reached home and I was relieved to find that same Auto-rickshaw driver waiting at our house. He was an honest man and brought my bag back, without looking into the contents. I felt like hugging him but resisted my urge. We silently exchanged hands and I gave him a handsome tip this time. He thanked me and left.

There was yet another incident which could have turned into a tragedy, because of my nature to easily get influence by claims of grandiosity, I went a local mechanic for checkup of our automatic transmission car and he fixed the wiring wrongly. While returning back home heard some crackling sounds and saw some sparks from under the bayonet and I took the fastest 'U' turn and went back to the workshop. He had asked to leave the car for a thorough checkup and we did. He was a cheater and a greedy man. He did the most unexpected transplant of our engine with some other customer's car and made a profitable deal. We brought back the car and noticed obnoxious consumption of petrol. Doctor suspected some foul play and notified it to the mechanic, who initially denied but, on our threat, to hand him over to police he accepted his crime and replaced our original engine. I promised myself not to go to him again. I had learnt a lesson and changed my outlook towards relying on boasters. Doctor's response to these mishaps was a simple phrase, that a person learns all his life.

RESTRICTED LIBERTIES

Only of late I understood why faith has allocated special rights for neighbors and why religion has covered repetitively in Holy book the concessions and grants meant to be showered as blessings towards neighbors. Our lives would have been a lot better without our related neighbors. Their formed opinions were biased and their embalmed sympathies were fake, their lodged loyalties were show offs, which didn't allow us to function above standard. Their affectations were becoming impossible to take anymore. They cannot be measured as any good relationships for closeness. To me these were unwanted cons given extra proportion of importance and our bending to please them was miserable foolishness and purchasable additional resentment, which was not worth any consideration. We allowed ourselves to suffer enough and maximally and we were searching possibilities to face realities then, not allowing them to escape their liabilities.

It became our continuous want to gain some understanding leave alone the relationship, which I was sure we will not get in time. A repetitive drama was created by these miscreants and they presentation has never ending asking response of protest from our side. I disapproved any humility in this regard and my perceptions were that of my sense of victimization. Good thing was we were accustomed to self-help and I started engaging in children's school activities, parent-teacher meetings, bank works of deposits and withdrawals, post office mailings and postage and payment of utility bills. I was even getting ready for routine official proceedings if required in the interest of family.

I was glad that children got into standardized schools with reputation in personality building and curiously girls got admissions by lottery and boy by influential contacts. Any normal person would have let me off the hook. One evening the younger one fell into sump and the neighbor boys only made some pretentious loud shouts, while a young man of our locality jumped and saved her before getting drowned. Even the demands of my household jobs were not enough to entice those people from expressing civilized reaction.

While they stayed home doing whatever they enjoyed I was blamed for irresponsible conduct and I forgot to go back and thank the savior and felt like going into bathroom and crying. Clearly, they were not nice people. I was wedged between our elderly in-laws including our related neighbors. Both were terrifying representatives of our present conditioned living. My younger kid looked as if she had accidentally fallen into hell.

The related neighbors were jealous of our slow resettlement in home land and expressed increased wants and materialistic demands. They arranged to steal our crockery, jewelry, stationary and clothing. I was getting rushed out of my tolerance but I remained intact, only slightly loosing my balance of reasoning at times and started peeping into jammed recesses of hopes which were slim and half destroyed and blocked them with concrete. I couldn't help except watching the events with lack of delight, added with little disgust but at least I was conscious of stands to be taken from now on, without getting influenced by their unconvincing melodrama. Doctor's claims of probable outcomes were incorrect and his advisories getting nullified into trivialities.

My sincerity was questioned time and again along with our concentrations on little things and my lack of control over mishaps. It was overwhelming to react over such overcrowded fabrications and I was aware that their sarcasms have no impacts to be pleased. I felt the attached pains, associated sufferings and demanded verification, but the resultant fumes were outrageous, words uttered hopelessly and exactions severed the relationship further. My provocations were kept shut, registries were ignored and curiously unendurable guilt was imposed on me with false talks conferring defamations only. All civilities were questioned from Doctor's side and all subtleties were answered from my side. I was getting an intuitive desire not to listen to these subjects, but I couldn't resist my urges to highlight my courage and self-confidence.

They couldn't have taken me as a mother with questionable maternal instincts to unearth antique blames, in spite of appreciating the spectacle, which they can see from close range. It would remain debatable as to who is more wrathful. My mother-in-law commented as to whether I realize that I could hold a baby while cooking, as she used to do and the looks she gave along-side, could splinter wood. I was not going to miss the opportunity and just stand listening like an irate actor. I was also well endowed in this department of para-phrasing, as I have given birth and raised three children already. I even ignored the drool of the youngster on my shoulder. Doctor's manners in this field were in progress. He was not very promising in the career of infant care. He wanted to say that embracing young mothers and chuckling infants is now part of his job description.

At least Doctor was nice enough to make an effort to attempt working out of his comfort zone. I was not hard of hearing and I could have lost grip towards wit and humor. Doctor thrusted his hand into his hair and looked away from me. I refused to be softened by the imagination, whether he looked as handsome as he wanted to be which was not going to change his behavior in general. On the contrary I took it as a clear insult, which could make me re-evaluate my chances of companionship for the rest of my life. It was his gesture that counted, after his own encouragement, more than his words. I knew I have to get used to it, but when we were all by ourselves his voice was surprisingly soft and mild. I excused him with a polite smile as an offering of my sincere sympathies towards him.

I resumed the normal routine of the prescribed duties and started to concentrate on my breathing exercises, which were useful tools as I found them, which were taught to me by Doctor himself. I felt I am regaining my composure. That air of impatience had gone but my body language remained as that of a reluctant recumbent unfortunate female. I was obviously making an attempt to hold my tears and be ready to dash my head to the nearest wall. I wanted to avoid becoming the iciest female. I didn't tell myself that I am habitually playing my role with modesty. It was the oddity of the situation that mattered and the oddity was seemingly making my situation worst. I wanted desperately to change the subject. My mind was getting enlightened by the early morning rays of light, coming from the east which should have given me some enlightenment and warmth.

The mistaken mishaps of the falsely arranged programs by Doctor in the confines of our bedroom were awful but also pleasurable, having been a part of life in the past, required forgiving and forgetfulness. I remember I shivered initially at the feel of strange movements with me and I used to automatically lean towards the extended provocation and suspended support. It was organically an awkward clinch for his benefit, while I was just role playing a catalyst. I had had that sneaky feeling that the surprised relaxation which followed was likened by the participants and appeared as a luxuriously coated experience for his solace, which simultaneously was soft and appealing to me as well. It was an endless ritual of performances going noticed or not, for which I hadn't had the time to stop and breathe and pamper my own wishes.

My formal or informal meetings with acquaintances meant for the solace of driving the pent-up frustration and for the good cause of passing time, in Doctor's absence went beyond repair. Later went out of proportion in normal setup of our relationship and that was not my fault. I was encouraged to do so. My quick retreat was not warranted by any social norms. I only could groan at the speculations of excuses and expressions uncalled for. I no doubt found myself safe among the hugging and cuddling of charismatic faces, that many love scenes find necessarily of paramount importance. Back tracking my resume, I could get reassured that I never had been a villain all my life, except an incident or two which could be ignored. I was intrigued by the inspected interest which followed my loved ones and got abandoned later, on the basis for the need of the time and hormonal surges which were apt to incur.

My older offspring, studying in modern girl's school, with modern trends and modern social circles was bound to get confused to witness casual differences in scenes being enacted, indoors and at her school when different faces appear at the school gate to drop and pick the same girl and she had heard about divorces and re-marriages as often as her assembly drill in the mornings. She couldn't help reporting the matter to her Psychologist deputed for counselling the growing apprehensions and fears of growing children.

She called me to enquire about the insurgence of any disharmony or expected calamity in break up of our relationship. I couldn't explain to her the intricacies of the demands and the follow up, pulling the normalcy. That moment my eyes streamed against the opposing forces open widely to encounter the worst possible humiliation one could stand for. I resurrected the usual shields introduced to me at accustomed times, which were not memorable any longer.

The life altering colors faded in ominous looking gray shades as though a rainbow is still stuck in the sky even after the rain has stopped. I was too astonished to notice the lurking hands and trembling fingers and my cheeks with their dimple were getting ruddy with currents of heat and humidity surrounding me. It was overwhelming to note the embarrassments which followed, when strangers approached for apologies and gratitude skidding into gathering apprehensions now on my side, losing surprises with anticipated mannerism. Following with the less athletic pace and getting ticketed for the fun journeys and occasional accompanied drinks to quench the thirst, there were only few stands of loose hair on the forehead to be straightened.

I gave a troubled gaze and my heart sank with a hopeless message for the corrugated design tugged for my regrettable disappearance and the re-abrasive argument with Doctor and my imaginations turning out into a kind of repulsion. I was appalled and stammered a hesitant protest, as though a sharp finger is poking my consciousness for the sake of honest enquiry. It was a charitable attitude which would have served me right, when I was ready for a tentative shield settled for my protection. Feeling my muscles quirking within my fingers and my pulse humping in leaps, when the breeze whipped my skin and hair, I felt additionally guilty for the made-up scenes, not erected by myself. Stress was doing odd things with me for my low anxiety crescendo and depressive traits, which I knew I also have to live with.

My refuge was my teenager brother's untimely visits to help, my nieces company for small exchange of small talks, and my cousin brother-in-law's humorous remarks to lighten my mood and the Doctor's acquaintances of the other faith with mindful advices and helpful tips came to my rescue. My older girl helping in small errands and feeding the youngsters, while taking the third feeding bottle for herself were additional stress busters to me. But ultimately servant maids were hired and my work load was eased out to a big extent. I was getting some leisure time for myself to think and analyze my position and future interactions. I realized I should have felt the aftermath of pressures early enough to expect unusual reticence.

Doctor's casual attitude was piercing my cage as a warning and I wanted to direct my mind to something remote. From the perspective of my looks, people must have found an appeal if not charm and I knew people become less disturbing if kept in their mental frames and in my looks, I couldn't have helped the glaring difference. People's choices and likes differ from person to person. As such I was not going to lose my temper, raise my voice or tamper my feet on the ground in anger, metaphorically or literally. I chalked a simple plan to act like a hen who would resist any intrusion by anyone to let her eggs be touched. I kept my reserve with strangers, which was limited from the very beginning. It was like eating sausages giving preference over chocolate syrup, which was my weakness. I made a mental note of it for future transactions.

Doctor's cousin sister who was to get married to him, if fate had allowed, visited us. She was another model to be crowned a beauty queen in some contest. We took her for long rides and dinners in fancy restaurants. Her husband who accompanied us very rarely was a docile man which was no company to count upon. But the lady herself was jovial and heart warming person. Kind and considerate at the same time. Smart and intelligent to add some credit to her personality. Aesthetically the prettier, in two dimensions I was best suited for a portrait to hung on wall, she was attractive on three dimensions to be ready to jump up in anyone's bed. Unfortunately, Doctor's bed with me inclusive was a luxurious resort for her, during her visit.

FORBIDDEN ENCOUNTERS

Not that I was a fortune teller, by it so happened that whatever I predicted did take place. I presumed it was my sixth sense and believed it. My sixth sense was about to forecast a small incident the following weekend. Life wasn't eventless and it was converted into some mishaps and some expected happenings. Doctor managed to purchase some properties in the suburbs and said, they would come handy in times of needs. One of it was on a hill resort and it was basically owned by another Doctor, who left his career practice and went into real estate business and was doing better. He had become very affluent as the city limits was expanding and people's choices were enlarging. His assistant approached Doctor and we all went to inspect the site. The place was plotted out and they were constructing the amusement areas. Winding roads were being excavated and ready to be paved. The assistant coaxed us to ride up the hill and Doctor declined, but I was interested. Doctor allowed me to venture and nodded the assistant to carry me.

He brought a motor bike instead of car, which he owned and offered it to Doctor, who waved his hand asking us to go ahead and he asked me to jump on the back seat. My reluctance was coaxed by Doctor, as he knew the roads were unmade and dusty to risk riding on four wheels. He remained beside the pool with kids and I adjusted myself to get on the back seat. The motor bike took a take-off and I had to grab the assistant to prevent falling out. He took the advantage and rode rashly over-speeding and the twists and turns of the dirt road were fearful but exciting. I couldn't help holding his waist tightly and he was in no moods to end the journey. Not that he was also enjoying the ride, instead he was enjoying my grip. It gave him more leverage as though he was given a green signal almost ready to somersault. We waved back down hill to kids, who were watching in amazement as we circled in and out of sight.

Incidentally I was wearing a single thick pleat swirled into a long hair strand, as thick as a broom, which was jumping shoulders, from me to the driver. The dirt road bumps and ditches were making me to lean on the assistant for support, with out realizing how this was affecting his nerves. The nerves of a bachelor deprived of norms and accidently got hold of the company of a full-bodied female clinging to his back, which was probably misunderstood. It was easy to lose sight of reality and as in old time phrase sentiment of courtesy, but I somehow escape the ride and exited without delivering my emotions. I was almost breathless with heat rising to show off on my reddening cheeks. I think I carried myself too far in the pretense with that stranger now preoccupied with impenetrable thoughts.

I never expected him to elbow punches in my waist hoping to go down my legs. I could have prepared a frosty armored shell if I would have known. But I angled him with a flirtish smile not hiding my feelings of joy ride as though I was in giant wheel of an amusement park. He misunderstood it completely. I was losing my patience. The ride should have been transient and short listed. I would have been happier with my pleated hair lying on my chest, but a flush rose up my cheeks when I imagined its dancing around people, known or unknown. I wasn't sure I had given enough credit and I lightly pulled on the end of my plait getting nowhere. I felt my skin was prickly under the pressure of forced clinging and I delicately shifted to ease the tension. Too many applications of touches had worked in the end. My facial expressions looked better than before. It was soothing to realize that there were no vacant gazes at my back. My limits were reaching breaking points with underlying embarrassments.

When we became stationary and exchanged pleasantries of good byes I came into open and even felt my back stuck with my life partner, while we could take another motor bike ride in the middle of the night. My thoughts were still engraved on my face and I was tempted to laugh aloud but I was exhausted by the grim silence from Doctors side. We were bored with silence, even seem unprepared for small talk, which I was afraid may deteriorate into an argument. I knew it was our premorbid types, which may rub or grind in attempts to break silence.

Doctor as usual was tapping the fuel indicator and the steering wheel in turn, whenever we are stuck in traffic. I wished I should have been driving instead and in which case I would have switched on the tape recorder to some old-time melodies for his amusement. I took a quite long sigh as an exasperation. Then I stretched my calf muscles and flexed my ankles. It was a good thing that I could anticipate his next move, my fragile system might not take it lightly. His side profile looked like a warning sign for me to maintain silence. The exchanged words would have been empty with emotions and silence was preferred, more preferably than sane people talking.

But I was worried for nothing as it unfolded later when we reached home, that Doctor was thoughtful and rather worried about his decision to shift from field work to teaching. Both had their plus and minus points. Still the decision was to be taken as on one side he would gain 10 years of time for retirement. I hummed to myself with a mouthful of fresh air, otherwise I could have been a tightfitting cork of a bottle. But it was not the most helpful gesture anyone would like at that moment. I think I was temperamentally not compatible at that time. My comparison of mind side stepped the norms. I wanted strong cup of coffee or an afternoon nap otherwise. My latest model was to remain obscure and disinterested, which I tried and failed. I smiled to myself looking into my reflection.

Life otherwise was on routine. Doctor attempted on private practice and very early decided to wind up. He instead ventured in construction activity on an otherwise dead project, brought to life and sold out the apartments holding one on his name. The dead project took some time but the result was rewarding. Children were doing well and he shifted to teaching line. I was not happy to be called a teacher's wife instead of Doctor's wife. But the compensations were plenty of holidays excluding seasonal vacations. We had plenty of time for ourselves and plenty of invitations from pharmaceutical sponsors to attend conferences, with all found including travel expenses free, boarding and lodging available at the venue for free and also free gifts to add to our collections. It was a privilege one would always welcome. The returns which pharmaceutical companies get is by Doctor's writing their branded products. No harm done to either side. In one of the conferences somewhere in south, one executive of some company also was available to receive and entertain guests. He apparently gave a lot of respect to Doctor and lot of attention to me. This time we left children back home for want of their preparation for exams, an untimely organized conference.

I found a lot of change in Doctor, as it was me alone he had to attend to and no distractions elsewhere. We used to loiter in the hotel holding hand and brushing lips to each other's ears, not exactly whispering. The executive was curious towards us and more towards me. He kept coming to ask for any service or help or favor for nothing. I think he was finding excuses to be around us. Doctor was pleasant in dealings with him, he being our host and apparently taking good care of us. In the evenings we crossed many times in the lobby or restaurant section and he was always found gazing at me. His obvious interest was noticeable, but I pretended not to recognize it. One evening we were lying down on couch beside each other and fondling with ourselves that he entered from the open door and notified about next day's program. Doctor took it easily but I was bit embarrassed and it showed on my face. He mistook as my appreciation towards him. No doubt he was good looking.

Next day while Doctor was attending his faculty meeting and I was in front of dressing table selecting my dresses to suit the expected gathering, that he entered the narrow corridor and came behind him and held me from the back with his hands grasping my waist. It was a surprise and my teeth made an audible sound. Ostensibly it is obviously an infantile gesture, as I could not find words for the occasion. I thought the less I say the less responsive I will become. Somehow, I suppressed the impulse to swing my left hand and slap it on his face, visible in the mirror. Presumably I just got blurred into one negligible composite, which was not me originally. I had the ability to control my body movements to go boneless effortlessly. He whacked the good manners, like a torn-out page of a magazine and interrupted midway through my vocalization by raising his grip moving upwards. I could only flip my wrist watch.

My vocabulary went out of mind's surface along with any sense of optimism. I wanted to jump at the sofa and clap for room service in absence of any. I reserved the right to twist my self out his grip and adjust the time depending upon when

Doctor may return. It was not the brightest of ideas for that morning, as I could not see any help coming from Doctor's side. I got into an illusion seemingly entwined between a teen agers curiosity and a grown women's sensibility, which I could differentiate at that moment. Hastily he left with a word that he is next door for any service. I fell down sprawled on the bed adjacent to the dressing table, head tilted to an angle, eyes half shut and wondered where from the executive could gather the courage to not just embrace me but also brush his body against mine in those brief moments. I reported the event to Doctor on his return and he looked vacantly and said to no body in particular that such things happen in life, which need not be given any importance, while I was wondering how I could let the event pass without protesting. He must have misunderstood me as a deprived wife without children and Doctor as a book worm occupied in research who has ignored my biological needs.

In no time he appeared at the door and wished Doctor, a very good morning and Doctor went to the door to converse with him about the agenda for next day. I could hear tiny whispers while glanced over my shoulder to find that chatting was friendly like animated characters of a cartoon movie. In the end I felt my moving out of his grip wasn't totally a loss. I had no compulsion to suppress my emotions and the misunderstanding is not going to be everlasting, as that of a lesser evil. I would have preferred a sulky silence over an indifferent one but chewing on his gum he eyed me critically looking over Doctor's shoulder and it interrupted my thought process. If things would have gone wrong, I would have been sucking my thumb like a girl of first grade. The story did not take a sardonic turn not to get a biting response from me, but I was biting my lower lip with upper incisors myself.

I didn't look at him sympathetically nor gave a patronizing hug to take him too far, but I risked my dignity anyway. He could have been back on his track overtly masculine, which otherwise would have been a compliment to him. But story ended into an anti-climax and next day evening we returned back. I knew he was not obliged to give a public apology for a brief private encounter between two unattached un-consenting adults. Perhaps he was unfamiliar with reciprocal expressions, otherwise he would have got an answer to the puzzle earlier. Good thing I had not given him any benefit of doubt, but he was totally responsible alone, as it was my implicated hypocrisy of some internal conflicts in my own misunderstandings. I was a grown-up woman, capable of my own decisions, whatever may be the response from the other side. It only denoted my popularity points.

I was an innate do-gooder now wondering what on earth that I did. I was becoming curious on self-reminders, that I had not leapt on him in self defense and that troubled my thoughts and reactions, which I was still holding on. I was mad at the outcome and it showed on my face as altered expression which kept him at some distance. I had been finding difficulty in keeping my facial expressions as blank as I could. I was unhappy. The streets looked gloomy, the façade of mountains behind the houses looked gloomy. I felt like I am walking alone in lurking isolation.

I couldn't have cupped Doctors face in the hollows of my palms to ignore the incident. I returned to bed, waited for Doctor to join to lower my voice in a husky tone but with persuasive intriguing edge, closed my eyes and distanced myself and then forgot it completely. Later Doctor explained that women reach their prime age after thirty, as they lose their inhibitions and start enjoying life as it comes to them. I failed to understand his logic or scientific word jargon but kept things to myself. There was nothing else which could have done any good from the past explorations. I was also prepared for the inevitable without losing my dignity, ready to pretend it as a fake encounter if need arise. I nervously crossed my feet and sat down as though I had no intention to get up at all.

DELIBERATE FANTASIES

What changed my perspective of life was three-dimensional cousin's re-arrival. Wasn't she making more visits than required? I knew she intended to marry Doctor if conditions and circumstances would have permitted their destined fates to shape up as they wished. But that doesn't justify any of this, in spite of she being a gentle lady and pretty faced with pleasant manners. I also knew she wouldn't hurt my or anybody's feelings against their will. I couldn't explain why stress was bubbling at the back of my mind. I wish I could control it before it leads into a nervous breakdown. Three-dimensional cousin came out of closed doors, where presumably Doctor was examining her low back ache, but Doctors always examine lady patients in presence of escorts. I was more interested to know how Doctor has perceived the unseen scenario behind closed doors. He was glad that she didn't have any evidence of lumbar disc prolapse. Well, it was self-assuring to her but not to me.

She left in urgency with side long glance and a half-hidden smile for making herself available for the follow up. I was about to start an in-depth analysis of Doctor's intentions, which could half-expectedly may turn out into an argument. I was appreciative of Doctor's patronizing smile at that time of scarcity and in the middle of an angry performance about to erupt from my side that the atmosphere navigated to a pleasant halt. I waited at the edge of the bed waiting for the inevitable to happen and I was imagining things to become intimate, so that I could create another love story of my own if time and need permit. I wasn't acting out, which otherwise could have been more fun. I was acting trying to bring back the balance after these emotional bumps of the recorded scene and off the screen. I was not actually dating with him and making a habit out of it.

My expressions on my face were meant for sensitive compassion and not fictitious blackmail. I felt the emotional surge in me and could even have been crude and blunt. I hesitated for a second, straightening my back which produced provocative invitation for him and even smiled for the sake of encouragement. I was waiting for any rating to be given by him on this and he took me to a new direction and an unexpected one, which I found very fulfilling and satisfactory. But I didn't know the follow up of the three-dimensional cousin would be so soon and on a working day morning when children were away studying and Doctor had an off, and we were still in bed. The servant maid acquainted with her, allowed her in and she could peep through our unlocked bed room. She was wearing an off-white Saree tied at the last support of her hip joint with a short low-cut blouse, which showed a lot. It looked as though, if she moved briskly the hip support will give way.

I watched her mischievous twinkle which caved on her. It was more like a decorative vase. With an audible intake of breath and smile widening she sat on the edge of my side of the bed, as though she wanted to reflect herself to be a Diva instead of human. I wondered how she could maintain such an hour-glass appearance on her waist. We had not even left the bed and brushed our teeth. She bent down and put her lipstick on my dimple, which I didn't mind because I had to wash my face anyway. She crossed her legs and leaned forward clasping her fingers around her raised knee. Her lips stick was showing her thirst for want of hydration. I got down to fetch a glass of water. Doctor's chivalrous gesture annoyed me. I had no desire to share even a second's company with any sentiment. I was left with a moment of self-pity to go to bathroom first to lose sight of them which was unacceptable, but I had initiated the move. I need to get back as I was allocated to be her escort, by the gesture of Doctor's hands and mission was next to impossible. I found it a pure challenge, even though no one was seeing the insidious ribbon of fear underneath, conceding to no further advantage. Doctor followed me into the bathroom and we were rubbing shoulders while brushing teeth.

When I returned back the white heap of cloth was lying beside the bed and three-dimensional cousin was on the bed covered under the bedsheet, as though ready for the follow up examination, of course there was no formal examination table in our bedroom. The scene was not disgusting and in ridiculous hope, less than an emergency, the prospect of sharing confidences of an escort was making me a weak link. Doctor's indifference wouldn't have been harder to handle, even in his bath robe, if not for his indifference in eyes, with which he looked at me. I knew any attempt to reconcile the situation would have foiled itself. I didn't know what would follow suit. Doctor held my hand, opened my fists and stretched my finger reassuringly. My nerves started subsiding into a gradual simmer. For all the flaws of my attitude at that moment, there was something still reassuring me. I went back and locked the door from inside for any unwanted intrusions.

What actually followed was very different, very unexpected, very uncommon, very unusual but not at all unpleasant, not very perturbing and not un-welcoming, rather I liked it and I fully enjoyed it to my absolute satisfaction. I didn't mind few additional pats on my back from both participants, for being so sportive and encouraging. I rolled my shoulders, stretching my arms and stood up. I was happily unstable on my feet for a while, which never happened before. All this was brought for the benefit of the participants not to utter few dialogues without a script in hand. We all came out of the bedroom, ate our breakfast and she was given ride back home. The sunshine was dim and the sky was dim looking too. I was relieved to note that I was not even remotely jealous about her. It was like a background shade cropping out from a shallow crater.

My reputation was also at stake but when I saw participants thoroughly enjoying the experience, I was not intending to play an innocent teen ager in any way and I fumbled around went back for a distraction from the rattling noise of rain falling on the window panes. It became little foggy and rain continued. To clean up the confusion in this issue, the point for consideration was that it was not an unholy alliance for cheating or fornication. My pride was not shattered to pieces, rather a confidence boost was made available by buffering a voluntary hand from my side and it was sentenced that no one is penalized or has become a barrel of laughs. Good thing I didn't cut them off for an inadequate apology not required and I had patience to be an equally responsible participant. I felt like wearing the beige color costume, which smelled like jasmine after the cologne it wore and be ready for Doctor's return.

Life came back to normalcy and my routine was repetitive with hauling the kids from their beds, helping them to get ready for their studies. My voice in pitch rising and falling and kid's eyes widening or narrowing depending upon the pitch. I got busy in the tasks of the social norms. Our friend also had to depart and she did but, not before introducing me to her distant relative who happened to be a shop owner of lady's garments in Lord bazar. I sense that she was trying to repay my favors. The shop owner was a fortune teller and knew a lot about palmistry. That was a subject of my interest and I welcomed it. One day during lunch recess I was there letting him read my future out of lines in my palm. He took my hand and on impulse squeezed it and started palpating the lines and the mounds, almost caressing my fingers, flexing and extending them. I deliberately poked my fingers in his abdomen and closed my fist when I realized that my fingers were becoming unsteady.

It was in reference to my reaction for having been manipulated by a stranger, even before he started telling my future. I pretended with out getting distracted that I believed him and awaited to be prompted by some good fortune in near future. It even brought me into a trance and I yielded to his manipulations. He pulled my hand and put it over his flexed thigh, as though needed light and concentration while going through my lines. As such I never believed in camouflaging a lot of acting out or make up. He could read dark circles around my eyes for lack of sleep in the past few days. He was a keen observer. I remained unmoved, except wiping sweat from my forehead by the other hand. I fixed my stare at him and found that he was also unmoved like me. The ante-room where we were sitting was large and airy. The three-dimensional cousin left us unescorted. He pulled me again and I lost balance on the stool in which I was sitting and landed on his lap dorsally.

I recovered my balance in utter disgust and weighed the chances of any long-term relationship with him. My defenses were professionally dissecting his intentions but not standardized. He apologized and I accepted his apology. There was no urgency to give any label to our relationship status with any name. there was intrusion by his acquaintance and he postponed the meeting and subsequent explanation for some other time and passed on a parcel before I left the shop. I kept getting illusions of his wants and needs from me as he was attracted by my appearance. It turned out to be a costly designer wear costume of purple color, which I admit I didn't dislike. Gifts always please me. More so if they are dresses of my measurements, which he took in person casually for his register, immaterial of the color choices. As a token of appreciation for his feelings I casually invited him to our house for a cup of tea and snacks. The known palmistry readout of my hand gave me a shivering which should have been hidden, but I made a poor job of it.

He came but at a wrong time, when Doctor was away again, children asleep and it was after early part of the night. He knocked instead of pressing the bell button and when I saw him it was evident, he wanted to avoid any company and had some malicious intent. I was almost rude to the extent wit and humor could be applied but opened to let him in the drawing room. He immediately grabbed me and showered his affection in a modern way, which I was not used to. I had some integrity I had maintained unlike others and unlike his acquaintance of three-dimensional cousin. I pushed and he pulled and I landed up on his lap ventrally this time but the drama was going out of hands. It was disgraceful for him to try taking chances this way. I was not programed in that manner as I had earned good-will points for nothing casual like this. With difficulty I tried a 'Mona Liza' smile without much success.

The plausible explanation could be that he was fed with wrong impressions out of recollections of our past encounters with our friend, the three-dimensional cousin. I cut off his exasperated rejoinder and the dramatic scene which he was expecting was not my choice or goal. I couldn't compromise with my feelings which were negligible but crept onto me that I couldn't recognize it earlier and in time. I wanted to be stern and firm in my standings and I couldn't be perspiring like a school girl in summer season, in spite of it being a summer night. I almost became a complete blank as though I was a statue in a wax museum. He understood that it was an unwelcomed interruption. He stopped his extensions as I was almost flattened like a punctured tire. He also noticed my narrow gaze, to avoid making a scene of itself. It doesn't usually come so easily. It follows a stream of protests uttered with out a sound.

My foundation, meant for cleansing before sleep also couldn't conceal my frown. Concealers can only do much. My color on my face was intimidating his grandiose approach. There was nothing soothing or comforting in it. I was no longer personally involved and I was agitated by this unwanted advantage he wanted to take out of me. I couldn't be dragged into any more trouble and I surrounded myself with a glass shield impenetrable. I was getting used to get things done my way, not the way anyone could use me like stuffed doll. I recollected how he had been percussing me while taking my measurements last time, he said just for future record, for order of some outfits on phone to avoid travelling from new city to old city, amidst menacing traffic. I knew I was played out and pointed my finger to the door, which he understood it as the final verdict against his passes and he left.

I notified the incident after Doctor's return from call duty and he kept his cool and got busy in the usual methods of his retirement to bed like any other day. I had lived with him for long to know him inside out. He as well must have anticipated some advances of this kind but he also had the art of concealing his layout in terms of emotions to be displayed for nothing, to be impacted. There is no dearth of chance mongers like the shop owner in this world. Only I couldn't be a part of it. I had enough on my mind with the happenings of my life to worry about such intruders. This is not the only sorrow to be purchased to pass time. I decided if I would meet him accidently again, I would not spare any gimmicks of separation anxiety any more, which was a solace to think about. There was no need for me to consult people like him for avoidance of conflicts which could blow out of proportion, if left unattended. I was sure he would be as complaining as I was with him, crossing limits of social norms with happily married women folk like me, who also can defend and protect themselves like liberated people, should remain a challenge.

WISDOM FOR WISE

Inspired by Allama Iqbal, a thinker, a scholar, a genius, an observer, an analyzer, a critic, an esteemed poet and philosopher of east instigated the partition of the sub-continent followed by masses immigrating either side. I wanted to interpret his thoughts, his conversation with God, as a believer of faith in a form of dialogue of his grievances to get the answers. He was the same nationalistic patriot who wrote the first national anthem after independence, but communal elements clipped with something else and also seeing the budding hatred and lack of secularism, he became a fundamentalist and edited this poetry which is still recollected by the people of faith in all the three countries which emerged thereafter. He remained sincere towards the wisdom preached by his faith and those lacked faced turmoil.

SHIKWA JAWABE SHIKWA became the wisdom for wise. This became an epic saga of sub-continent uttered in a rhyme and rhythm of poetic script on which he dared to complain to God and received reciprocal wisdom reprimanding to any explanation incomparable to any clarification warranted for the mankind in general and believers in particular. It transformed into a challenge bubbled with humility and God's addressing to believers with dignity became a collection of poetic verses of great significance and amalgamated into a height of intelligence if could be understood, would lead to wisdom. My stupidity allows me to do as much and any under doing or over doing require forgiveness, it couldn't have been appreciated by west in local dialect.

It quotes to God, I have to say maybe out of distortions of my mind and out of belief in you. Tell me as to why I should remain silent waiting for your enlightenment to get to me and continue avoiding the norms of present day society around me. Why shouldn't I avail the benefit of my interest earned from my savings which I don't wish to invest in recognized shares and which I found is risky as circumstances are collapsing for reasons I can't justify and as to why after so much foreground to play could leave me nothing for my rainy days and which I religiously believe and would continue to do so accordingly. I don't consider me a bud about to blossom showing concern for myself and my needs which are becoming un-predictable with passage of time. Why should I remain engrossed in selfish motivations like others, as though I am not finding the depth of gratitude of faith in your kindness and extended help all along towards believers, me being one of them.

Why should I remain attentive to keep listening to birds chattering in appraisal of your blessings also conveying their liberation and freedom, when I am roofed around with liabilities and obligations to serve your cause. I see birds flapping their wings and moving freely singing songs in you with applaud, around gardens full of color and aroma of sweet nectar coming from petals of the flowers blossoming to their maturity to captivate the tantalizing beauty in them portrayed by your graciousness, but I can't be one among them to just stay still and swing along the directions of the breezes of mornings or evenings or any times destined by you. I can't be a still art piece without emotions, I can't be an unopened flower bud hidden somewhere within me waiting to open and claim its existence. I have to raise my voice, my protest and my eruptions of thoughts to make myself heard.

I developed the courage to gather words to pronounce my anguish in the shape as that of my call, my appeal appearing as a complaint. I hold the fore bearing of tolerance to verbalize my gripe, as I feel it is mandatory with regards to the needs of the time. It has somehow shaped itself into a petition awaiting a verdict to become a sentence to get passed by your judgement of wisdom to denote whether I deserve the consequences. I admit and accept that we as believers had been involved in self-gratifications of our greed, and the mailing with gruesome desires which could tear apart anyone's feelings for our satisfaction.

Now I confess the time has come for me as a singular and believers as plural, to reach you and feel compelled to extend my deep-rooted sorrows, which make me cry being tragical and feel obliged to express my sadness to depict my helplessness and hopelessness, but I don't have any regrets with this confession of my agony and suffering to you and you alone, being dear to me and I am still trying to come closer to you. As of now I have no hesitation to register and identify that we are still occupied in pleasing others, pleasing people, people in authority, people whom we loved and trying to please those are beautifully dressed and pretty and not so pretty. We are also pleasing the poor, the needy, orphans and wayfarers and the people gone astray and the wrong doers. The rich and the homeless alike.

Do you think I can or we can help it? We can't, as we are captivated by the surrounding influences, captured by the enveloping system, the annulment and the condition in which we are living, the co-incidences we are facing, the selective choices we are left with, the selective honesty we could survive with, the selective sincerity we can accumulate, the selective shortcomings, handicaps and disabilities we are endured to bear. The instruments on which we used to crawl, walk and play and sing and feel good about are silent and still. We are left with no encouragement, no reciprocation and support and that is making us to feel dejected, obstructed and rejected in our efforts getting nullified and all this is making our hearts to get filled with imaginary thoughts, thrusting egos, evaporating obsessions and in the end leaving us to erupt volcanic lava with regrets.

And if we have to appeal, petition and seek refuge for our past status where can we go, whom could we approach, whom could we rely upon, lean upon, find shoulder to sob except you. We have no body to ask for and we have nothing at our disposal, except your mercy and graciousness. We have nothing to bank upon, to feel proud of and to get any favors from. So, we are dealing with you in direct connection that we may be exempted from your indifference and let us recoup for our losses which we incurred lately. Addressing to you directly please listen to these words, these statements these thoughts and these feelings from your believers, followers, slaves and servants. We had been the one who were and will continue to be praising you, adoring you, thanking you and loving you and trying to reach you for your attention and sympathy. Please give a moment to hear us, ones who feel so close to you that we dared to express our truth of invocations asking for your favor for listening to your believers, who are ourselves. You may not respond or reply if you so wish, but we are your own creations expecting your mercy.

There are no compulsions to answer and you are not obliged by your will, might and right, your grace, your dignity and your position and prestige and you may attend to this invocation in whatever way you feel is required to be done in this regard. I expect you to fulfill my needs, my wants in whatever way you think can satisfy me and us. It is not a complaint in literal sense it is a cry for help, but I still want you, my master my guardian, my savior to listen and solve this quest for my seeking the truth behind the happenings, in spite of the fact that I had been beholden of your compassion which you have been bestowing upon us up till now and hopefully would remain the same way. Forgive us if it is sounding anything else, which is crossing its limits and boundaries of ethics and etiquettes warranted from us.

Angels were astonished upon my approach of this unique kind. They wondered how come the voice from the earth could tear the skies and reach so high up. They found it perplexing that this secret which is unfolding its story by itself and the presentation so bold and clear, but obviously incompletely understood by the complainant in its purpose and meaningfulness be told in so many utterances. The residents of seven heavens along with angels and Jinn were amazed by the courage which the voice contained to be heard by God, actually coming from a slave among believers.

How come the human intellect could gather out of the lowest of the morality of their wisdom and pointing critically to the highest governance and how come this pinch of dust could set up a plan to make it a grievance to God almighty, with incompletely understood conceptions not recollecting the favors already showered on this race from God's beneficent role given to them all along from times immemorial. How this voice managed to reach so high with their tireless efforts to get God's attention, without they even recognizing the consequence.

The residents of the earth seem to be ignorant of the norms of adequacy and how could they forget the delicacies of attitude and behavior in devotion towards the creator, to whom they are supposed to commit and submit in totality. They believe they have a right to converse with the all-powerful almighty and protector of earth, galaxies and heavens. They have no sense of comprehension to apply and they have no idea how to verbalize in proportion and balance of difference of status they hold and the status God held for Himself.

God was wondering; how notorious and mischievous these people of low altitude have become. They seemed to have crossed the boundaries of faith restrictions and the warranted submission, that they are expressing their frustrations and antagonism towards God. Are these the same race who were grinded between angels and the super-naturals, as they are intoxicated with stupidity and intolerance unbecoming of their kind.

They are not aware of unbounded truth, predicated by the subdued secrets to which they have not yet been exposed. They are showing arrogance and pride in this attempt to converse with their master, by their fabricated strengths, while they are not even methodically trained to make sensible conversations and delicacies of norms they have been filtered and taught with, which is sheer ignorance than innocence.

God, we submit ourselves to your mercy and but please be informed that it was we the believers, who have erased the darkness from the pages which were trending and it were we who escorted the slaves from the doctrines of transgression prevailing around, it was we who have been prostrating to decorate your Holy Shrine by our foreheads bent down in prostration to let it get established in its recognition as you have pointed out that it deserves. It was we who have pasted the scriptures of the Holy Book on our chests holding them tightly closer to our hearts to get documented forever. But still we are blamed finger pointing towards us that we are not loyal or obedient to you and that got registered in your records then we humbly notify that you have not whole heartedly acknowledged these registries.

There are races and clans and people among whom there are sinners, and wrong doers, among them are taste mongers and egotism mongers, declaring themselves as self-righteous but they are not, among them there are people who are lethargic, lazy and retarded and maybe some fool hardy too or some intelligent and there are thousands who have gone astray and have no inclination or attachment with your significance. But you are showing your prize and showering your blessing on them and you are critical about us, who are still your believers and willing to obey you commands as religious duties. We are the ones who have followed your legacy of straight path, which is directed in the Holy Book. We are still remaining sub-servant towards your instructions some which are clear and some which are subdued.

Came back a thunderous voice that quotes, I am listening to your story and it appears laden with sadness and it also appears that you have over loaded yourself with sorrows which have filled up your capacity of bearing. Your words have crossed the skies and the presentation curiously interesting and your formulation of vocabulary manifest your heartfelt feelings with which you are living. It is blissful that you have vocalized the protest in a nice way to suit the realm of the predicted stretched norms which you tried in bringing this desirous conversation from earth to your master, who is all knowing and wise and by this you have opened a method to come into contact with your creator, sustainer and provider and forgiver of your misdeeds and sins from His bounty of mercy promised to you.

Continued..........................

WISDOM FOR WISE - 2 CONTINUED

The relevant parameters which you have not internalized and introspected are the questions which you have put not self-explanatory that who has erased the darkness to light for mankind and believers, who has saved the encaptivated from slavery to freedom, who have been putting their foreheads in prostration for the recognition of Holy Shrine and who have been embracing the Holy Book to their chests for its deserving position. They were your virtuous predecessors and not you. But as of you, where to do stand and what are your accomplishments. You are just *sitting cross handed awaiting redemption and our graciousness.*

I know my lord, my master that I have no courage or right to question your plans, programs and decisions, which were always favored your slaves by your shares in bountiful amounts you have kept in reserve, which are mostly unknown to us. But we want to know why believers are designated less fortunate in the pretext of worldly wealth, richness and position, available luxuries and comforts in this world. Your treasures are not insufficient, not less paramount in any way. The power which you behold could spring water fountains from the desert, your greatness has unaccountable blessing which could be scattered and no limit of your empowerment of wealth and gifts which you can distribute. You could bring rivers from mountains and plantations from ground with fruits for relishing and cherishing the wishes for all mankind.

We get a feeling that we are left with nothing but additional criticism, sarcasm and got lowered by degradedness. Is this is the reward we deserve after conveying, exhibiting and executing our refuge in you with our commitments of lives for your sake. We don't intend to compare the benefits others are deriving out of your graciousness, but they are directed to those who have no connection with you, have no capability to verbalize phrases in your praise or have any interest to reach you. And they are getting worldly paradise like recompenses and we are only being given promises of rewards in afterlife. We feel deprived of your love, sympathy, trust and escort and consequently are we partialized by defeat, victimization and hardships only. What has gone wrong with our righteous deeds, and tests on walking on the prescribed right path advocated by your Holy Book's directives and why we are not simply getting what we also should get.

Listen oh! Believers, now that you have opened to spell, let it be known to you that your preachers are no more lodging the abstract wisdom required from their side, they don't carry the electrifying principle in their impulsive meaningful behavior, their recitations are lacking in appropriate explanations, and also lacking in conviction they are supposed to behold. What is being heard is the call for prayers without the soulful depth in it which should spread and you are responding with the expected philosophy influenced with our interpreting the true sense of the same, leaving behind the wanted containment it should carry. Mosques are crying out for the company of true prostrators, genuine for the faith prerequisites of correct guidance and entry without gratitude and gratefulness necessary from you and you dare to claim that only the benefits of heavenly promises are being passed on to your future.

If you are bent upon countenance then apply logic and reasoning to it. There should also be maturity of thought you contemporarily present and sincerity of affectations you need to pass on. Have you speculated that from times immemorial rules are adjudicated to regulations which are binding on all.

But now that you are unhappy and disappointed about non-believers being placed better than you in regards to our gifts, the fact remains that you have not been longing for the same and you are unwilling to put in efforts to get the fruits of your labor, which you were supposed to. It is mandatory that performances have to be displayed before awaiting the results.

The blessings given to your predecessors is still lingering on but you are unlike them. Rather you are ignorant of essential arts and crafts, devoid of eminent learning and qualifications and you are uninterested and less bothered about the incidences taking place in your own homes, which you are obliged to control. The crucial roofing required for your shelters is weak and it is apprehended that if you are provided a chance you may sell your faith and that of your predecessors for petty returns.

You may not hesitate even to trade off the knowledge given to you and in great probability you may sell the idols and the material focusses, reconstituting as loved objects and bank upon them for small profits. You should know that the purpose of your existence is to franchise that your race in one, that is singular and that is because God is singular, His prophet is singular, His preached religion of monotheism is singular, the Holy Shrine is singular, the Holy Book is singular then you all should have been one.

I would have been satisfied and judicious if the believers should have been singular, as one in all aspects of commonness and its mythology. On the contrary you are split in groups, sects, castes and creeds of followers distinct in your own existence practicing communalism among yourselves, which is now prevalent. Do you think this is the way lives of believers should be lived? It appears ridiculous.

Oh God, they say that believers have gone into idolism and they are happy that guards of Holy Shrine have vanished in darkness, even when you spilled light and food carried on caravans meant for us and we acknowledge all and are still sticking to the Holy scriptures which are meaningful and purposeful, which is not being stacked on the other side. We are not sure whether we have highlighted the delicate discrimination of your authority and your bounty.

It is known that believers have departed from the world, we think they never existed among you of these times, and they have not been the same as they should have been. You are comparable to Roman Catholics, traditionally you are somebody else, the old time Egyptian Jews may feel ashamed of you and your practices and you people have allotted ambiguous amenities to yourself to safeguard your identities for name sake. You are different than what believers should be.

Every believer used to be weapon against the transgressors, they had the tact and talent to impose justice and righteousness, they were dependent on their strengths to shoulder their responsibilities, while you are afraid of death they were afraid of God. If you are not carrying the genes of them to your progeny then how would this race can inherit the required guidance for the straight path lime lighted on to you. Every one of you is seeking your own goals in your own comfort zones.

This is not the way one could survive. You lack the wealth of your predecessors and the depth of spirituality they possessed. They were respected for their forte of belief in truth and you have gone astray in spite of notarized teachings of the Holy Book.

You prefer avoidance for escape and they were strugglers of peace maintenance. They were ready to embark themselves for the good cause of balance but you would try running away. You are only conversant of small talks when they were true followers of the commission. You are aspiring for buds and flowers, when they had gardens in their custody.

We testify that we are in total submission to your glory, compassion and beneficent magnums shown to us since long and hopefully would continue. We are stranded in gardens sketched with colors and fragrance awaiting your approval and grants, which is awaited by the rhymes and rhythms of contentment for our satiety and satisfaction. We want to be far away from the turmoil of conflicts and indifferences and express craving for your favors. We are circling around the candle of light like insects, groping for warmth and brightness in between the dark alleys and we are wishful to leave our dormant status to be overcome by your wisdom and supervision. Give us some help and support to let us overcome our fatigue and weakness to recover back our strengths as we are still your slaves and believers.

Now don't get excited out of the colors of gardens surrounding you, the branches of the trees will sparkle with new buds to blossom into flowers of fragrance and your dedication is a necessity to fill up the absence of your attendance in gardens of paradise. The red shades depict the sacrifices of martyrs who have given their lives in our cause, of propagation of truth meant in the message of the words In Holy Book.

The dust around is shaded with gray which will shine to glittering rays sparkling with embellishments. Don't get harassed by the present chaos you have landed into on your own accord but you will sail from sand to shore and turn the waves into storms by your belief in faith and you can uplift yourselves to heights of glory and success.

Be judicious and righteous in your deeds and commit to predetermined victory, which is inevitable and if you remain faithful to the last sent prophet for your call then we are always with you. We will sanction more than this world, and bless you with the pen and the graphics of authority which you can enjoy in history forever. Thus, be rest assured of the given word and remain true believers.

Oh! God the most gracious and the most merciful, I am the author of this book addressing to you this time. I don't know what Allama Iqbal intended by writing 'Shikwa Jawabe Shikwa' and how you perceived his oration in this regard, in spite of the fact that I know he was a genius and I am not, but Doctor appreciated his poetic recitation and I was impressed, as it was in the local sub-continental dialect, but if there are errors you feel are outrageous in my translation of it, I seek forgiveness for that.

You are my master and I am your slave and will remain so all my life continuing to seek refuge in your guidance and mercy, for I know we all have different variations in our faith levels, but all pointing to your perfection and precision. You have demarcated earth and sky and kept a harmony in both. I understand the overall message of your quotes and interpret it as parable and analogy to water raining from sky to earth. The water is pure and the Holy scripture is pure, the water has the potential of transforming the dry earth to greenery, all being an incredible change amounting to a revolution, which is meant for transformation.

I could grasp the meaning of your names, four out of ninety-nine mentioned in the Holy book. You are the king and protocol behind it is me to submit to you in totality and I cannot walk out from you. You're the authority beholding the dignity and respect and I am drawn towards you with loyalty. You are pure, free of flaws and full of refinement and I am gravitating towards you and you are wise and sought after, being a mentor and a guide and I cherish every moment to be in your company.

Your first two names are belittling me and I am intimidated by the same but simultaneously the following two names bring ease and solace to me and I feel closer, intimate with you and I think that is how you wanted to keep a balance for our guidance. Your message of the Holy book, which is a miracle sent to humanity by your last messenger passes on an endless wisdom from those time to eternity of the eras which will follow and I abide by this message for its spiritual and moral benefits. Please forgive any oversights, mistakes and sins committed by me in error in the past.

Not that I intend to find fault with Doctor but most of my life I was governed by his vision of what life should be and I hope he corrects himself in introspection, insight and invocation in future. I also seek forgiveness for him and for my family, as to err is human, to repent is human and to transform is believer's liability.

Author in humility.

GLORIFIED FAILURES

It proved itself one day. I found nothing more intriguing than whispers which were thrown long back for my hearing and I was not able to follow their direction. It was true that I was not very familiar with desperate sucking of air into my abused lungs, by passive smoking from Doctor's pipe, which was in a sense my unfortunate incapacity, otherwise to have found it earlier, which I could have done at ease on my own hopelessness to get reduced later. While cleaning and dusting the shelves of my wardrobe my old-time journal and the diary, in which I used to write my feelings fell down on my feet. A corner of an envelope was peeping out of the inside of its leather cover. I casually lifted it to note that it was a note in Doctor's handwriting meant for no one except me, may be inspired by some poet like A. Faraz, which of course got missed out its contents, which upon reading and re-reading I felt I would be better off doing some deep muscular relaxation techniques or some yoga stretches to perceive some coolness unfazed. It depicted the following:

Loved one,

It is known that people look at your beauty wide-eyed, then let's stay in your town to see how mesmerizing are your looks. It is also known that your beauty has a sympathetic eye towards the down-trodden, then let's destroy ourselves to be able to get some attention from your side.

Heard that your gracious glances go the extent of purchasing pain and suffering for the desirous then let's bypass your lane to seek your comforting gaze. Also heard that you have some courtesies for poetry, in appraisal of your prettiness then let's see the miracles of our talent hidden in it.

It is told that flowers scatter around when your lips move to resound some words, then let's see the results of a conversation with you to get what is wanted. It is told that moon stares at you with continuity in the nights for appreciation to your comparable elegance and stars bow down from the horizons to get a glance of it.

It is notified that butter flies surround and tease you in the day's light and fire flies take halts in the darkness in want to see the clarity of your appeal. It is notified that the charm of the blackness in color of your eyes is in itself forecasting the doom in it, so the cosmetics meant to enhance the loveliness of eyes will take sighs of amazement of your eyes.

It is believed that your deer like eyes are a disaster in itself for the onlookers and their exquisiteness is exasperating for some, so deer are magically charmed upon looking at them. It is also believed that your cute features are a mirror reflecting your attractiveness, so even humble people groom and dress appropriately to watch to see you closely.

It is denoted that the captivating curves and contours of your beauty are so alluring that flowers had to cut their petals to upgrade their standardized shapes to match up with you. It is denoted that paradise is adjacent in equality to your presence of a garden, that allows the residents of paradise to have double views of enchantment on both sides.

And your passive glances and subdued smiles can demolish the caravans of love and want for you and subsequently the beholders of such emotions would look at you in fear and intimidation.

It was declared tat red roses envy the tender freshness of your lips, then resultantly the spring has to be blamed for creating the same antiquity of purpose, which has created this rivalry

It is documented that if you stay still, the natures movements circumvolute around your posture and when you move the eras stop to gaze back at you. It is inevitable that no one is blessed to see you bare, in the way nature creates beauty and presumably only the walls and doors of your den may be lucky to get a glance of it at times.

Let all these be stories or dreams in exaggeration of your profile, it is worth interpretation of those dreams for searching the ground realities. Now whether to stay close to you forever or to move across the journey and to leave your presence, which then would become mandatory to leave my search and desire for you in transit against my intentions.

Admirer

It was all a reflection of ironically presented words, phrases and paradigms that made me to feel a half-convinced self to be enjoying the absurdity of the facts, which went through my life all this long. I also thought it lacks love and holds an excess of lust and I was also observing the mania with perplexity, half-yielding myself to the past. I was thinking like a pessimist, who refuses to believe the predictions of feelings felt in the past, present or future, as the contents were un-dated and were not showed to me on any specific purpose. I was feeling tired then and there. I felt lying down and

I was overtaken by painstakingly curled up sleep, while rain stuttered on the roof. I was getting saturated by my own doubts and I tried to convince me that I could be wrong and I was proved wrong when I was getting hypnogogic hallucinations about Doctor waking me up very tenderly and I woke up. Doctor understood my mental state and informed me that it was written long back.

He went further to tell me that he has one more for future and went back to get yet another envelop, sealed for me to open later. He lied low and caressed my back. He whispered something in audible words, which I couldn't comprehend fully, but I knew his intentions and was not fully prepared for it. As far as I new it was not a prior agreement in the list of the activities dedicated for the day. I also knew he is trying to pin me down. I felt justifiably annoyed to note that my face was turning red without an admixture of white to turn it into pink.

I yielded and even enquired about the opened envelope. Doctor was completely at ease, rather relaxed and didn't bother to respond. He almost pretended as though he has not heard and seemed preoccupied evidently on the status of global warming instead. I failed to swap the necessity of replacing his characteristics on the sidelines. I looked lie a cheerleader of the team facing the worst defeat. Deep inside I was dancing a tribal dance from one foot to another, pleased unnecessarily for some made up reasons.

The second envelop seemed to be the lesser of the two evils. It was cold outside I was feeling warm inside. It was difficult to recall rotations of days and nights, revolutions of many years spent in companionship of ups and downs, happiness and sorrows. What was comforting that he had brought me to new levels of interactions with no disturbing feelings for each other. Before I could completely lose grip over the situation, he swept me into his arms but it appeared a cheeky squeeze, which earned him a pinch in his arm. There were other successful ways of the cuddle, in which one could anticipate the other persons reaction. My good riddance attitude over the open envelope clearly propagated. It was one of the fake smiles I could manufacture on my face, which was not easy. I was actually pretending to be someone else, which was not my regular habit. From a critical point of view the embrace was stiff un-becoming of Doctor's type, lacking in any chemistry.

On the next available opportunity, I couldn't resist the urge to open the last envelope given to me and retired on sofa to read it. It said in so many words:

My companion and my life partner,

Beyond doubt you had been my soulmate all my life and we had a very gratifying and fulfilling exchange of solace among ourselves, which cannot be erased from my memory, duly imprinted for good. But now you can't expect me to part with my previous extensions and cannot share the same intensity of affection, which I could do so in the past. There are other distractions which are inviting me to inspect and resurrect other than the pleasures of your companionship which we cherished up till now.

I was mistakenly undertaken the impression for quite a while even until of late that if you are just remaining beside me, it may suffice the cause and effect of the purpose of life for me. Your connectivity if remains consistent with me, then I don't even have to worry towards the left-over life span's hardships and struggles which seem inevitable and now even becoming evident with the passage of time.

I acknowledge that the grace and glamour of your personality is sufficient for me to forgo springs and its blessings, without accepting defeat. There is nothing left for me in this world except the coziness of your glances and incarnating glares for me to last forever. I am on the verge to decide that now that I still have you inside me, the destiny has befallen a blessing on me.

But don't ask for the same returns from me, which I am not capable to give you in possible future. The legacy of history as it reveals itself with unaccountable years of our togetherness I lasted in your company as if our lives were woven in fabrics of satin, velvet and chiffon knitted together to cover us in totality.

But the fact of the matter which has taken a turn is that at every nook and corner of streets and market places, I find bodies young and not so young which are put for sale, swept in dust and dirt and bathed in blood and I can't help looking towards these atrocities they are subjected to, asking for my attention depicting real tragedies of this world.

It is undisputable that I still find your beauty appealing and captivating to me, but now that I have to evaluate where I should be inclined, whether in the direction of this appalling havoc around or the pleasure which we shared, the mutual liking we enjoyed and the good things which we jointly adored. But I am afraid I am not in that happy position to share with you all the past in future.

Yours not any more.

A realization got dawned on me that time will never be the same as it used to be. Change follows towards the better or worst which needs to be identified and recognized as an eventual fact. According to the saying wishing well make it happen, I started counting on the odds which may be faced in the indeterminable time to come and whether I would be able to face it all by myself. With his pending commitments to be met with as liabilities and to be fulfilled religiously was making me to act reasonable. He took some tentative steps in the direction for a good cause and seem trying to push time away, made me live some moments of anguish. He thought the healing process will scar the wounds and I was thinking every thing is going off the track, leaving me with sensitive negotiations for which I was left with a mixture of unhappiness and despair.

In spite of the charms which could be gathered from the left-over memories I was not able to proclaim any benefit as encouragement to live other than getting harassed. My plausibility lent its conviction based on my genuine apprehensions, but his predatory intent was declared final, without a liaison and has been drawn towards his desires which could not have been understood by me. I was getting aware that I still could give my years of experience for these moments to get frozen. He still had responsibilities towards me and the well-being of family and he could not walk out as a favorable option. I thought he has gotten tired of everything and is afraid to admit sensibly for God's help to come to his resue.

No suggestions appeared conspicuous which were simply formed and were absolutely unnecessary. But what was declared was ambiguous with discrepancy lodged in it, a draft of an unwritten document without signatures and no explanations could be given of any pronounced enhancement. I decided I will apologise on his behalf for his inappropriateness in dealing with sympathies. Incompletely understood entanglements and a sense of indolence will sail with his dictatorial options and last irrevocable judgements. I couldn't take any confidential discussions after the disclosure. I will have to restrict myself to suggestions, concise, and astute.

It was clear that it was an unwritten but understood theme with no chance for any anticipatory counter suggestions. If I could trace the sequence of events from place to place, it would not lighten the oppressive atmosphere which was created and now surrounding me. I felt myself to be a persuasive inmate of a prison despite crime being delegated to Doctor's name and I had no obligations to mix ingredients and measure his critical remedies for approval by the allocated system. He has to do that himself, as it was his liability and not mine.

HARMONIOUS DISCORD

It was far more graphic than the designated limits of my tolerance. Tolerance to my stupidity or tolerance to his outrageous wisdom. I could not allow Doctor's logic to his pleas which was attending beyond my cry for help. In my judgements it was his altered ego, which did not even lead to any delicate balance and would have exploded under paramount conditions of adversity. It was making me to work virtually under impossible circumstances. Doctor with his linguistic flaws soft or hard had deliberate tempo started manifesting its results. But I felt there was no point in going into past errors or present mistakes. Recitations had to be brief, crucial to understand and without backlogs to be left for repetitive corrections. I had a mind set to remain contended and my limited experience to bank upon so, I had to pursue specific ruminations not previously brought for debate.

Half the time I was answering my own questions, trying to refine countless details which I didn't want reluctant audience to listen and then get charged with relentless emotions. I was groping for incredible and unthinkable solutions to my problems, problem of great magnifications if magnified under microscope or watched as distant hopes to get faded from a telescope. I was not inclined to hold any convocations or to pass verdicts on illogical judgements. Doctor had as always trying his level best to demand petulant gratifications of his needs, getting annoyed on the critical opinions about his motives and getting embarrassed on his outbursts of insanity, being a product of his own shortcomings. He was definitely getting tired and was frightened to remain within sanity which of course didn't come to his rescue. This time he wrote an open letter not enclosed in any envelop for me to read.

My love of life,

A time seem soon to arrive when you may not find me in your company any more, but there will be no dearth of others to seek your company to find solace in gratifications of their motives and cravings even malingering to be in appreciation of your care, concern and considerations. There will be no dearth in scarcity of pleasure seekers who would adore your empathy towards them, except me.

I am overwhelmed by your discrete negligence for me, your deliberate distancing and distraction in matters of importance for yourself. And there is world of sorrows I am enslaved to live with and additionally the single sorrow of your continued liability on me. Alone in its gravity that single sorrow is weighed against multitude of sorrows which I could have lived with and this alone is an enough suffocating evidence for me to die.

Just in case I vanish from this earth and your life for ever and for good, the grief of my separation will not heal the leftover scars of the open wounds for you to recollect and bear with them. The irreparable damage accompanied by pain of this separation will be intolerable for you to bear with.

The turmoil of conflicts of interests with which we lived till date and may have been living with those contractions to accept and live, I am afraid will ever have conjoint consultations and compromises to find a solution out of them.

The advocacy of the remnant facts speaks for themselves and would remain so that I will have my own grievances with your mind set and patterns of thinking which will in the end may become so grave and debilitating that in comparison you may not find space and time to express your annoyance and agitation against me.

Even if I do not remain with you close and passionate anymore, I will pray that you find others to replace me, without even noticing my absence. It will not be the company alone but the truth associated with the company you may hold of others involvement will provoke the genuine answers which were a requirement in our exchanged relationship.

And be informed that if and once for all if, we get separated in literal sense then we would meet in each other's dreams like one finds a shrunken dried flower stamped amidst the pages of old scriptures in books.

Neither you are a lesser god neither I am a lesser evil, even our mutual likeness towards each other is not equal to the connections between angels and the God. Both of us are human, mortals and ordinary beings so, why we should even attempt to meet between curtains of veils, which cannot be defined.

The sorrows of the world may better be amalgamated with the sorrows of our expected mishaps of separation, as the intoxications of the intoxicating drinks increase many folds upon getting mixed.

Let us search loyalties among the destructed and destroyed people, as these treasures are discovered in the absences and inhibitions among ourselves. Neither I have remained the old self nor you have remained your own self or our past can be relived so, like two shadows merge in mirages of the desert, we will accept our destined fates.

But what a turmoil you inflicted on me, by restraining your feelings from getting exposed in spite of me severing your loyalties which you had been extending towards me all along and even now you accepted it as a well-wishing gesture, which to me is like a drunkard who exceeded boundaries of antiquity, shows off by abstinence and even without intending to drink any further continues to hold the glass in hands.

In our garden of domicile spring comes and vanishes in no time but you kept your mindset with ingenuity and was cautious in not verbalizing your grievances and the message which became expressive behind the crevices of your mind as I read, was your silence and refraining from seeking answers to the leading questions and you did not utter a word and kept feelings to yourself, which was your type.

Yours truly.

I knew Doctor was trying to implicate me in any of my conceivable wrong doings and my erroneous duplicity and was trying to pronounce the unpronounceable fears to make them perfectly amenable by imparting reasonable excuses, which I was not able to make peace within myself. I was left to helplessly straighten out the built-in risks and responsibility without knowledge and his domineering authority to be resented willingly or unwillingly, all be lingering under the influence of inspirations one gets out of poetry. His motives were certifiably insane as he was trying to pretend to be offensive in his own defensive capabilities. His usual responses including this to my flow of requests from past into present going into possibilities of future were beyond common understanding making no substantive change in our stands thereby making our relationship very delicately poised to become unstable.

Doctor had some peculiar ideas of norms invented as self-made biographies. He would be in favor of celebrating Birthdays after 20 years of age, opinioned as a doctrine that if we do so then we are admitting that we don't want to grow up. 'B' days in his opinion are for kids to make believe that parents celebrate their births and are proud about it. He used to take the major decisions of life and he would allow me to take the minor one and I was curiously happy for the same. Decision making on important issues hold immense responsibilities if they go wrong. He wanted his children to become independent and were given liberties to take their career selections and partner selections on their own. Children were doing well in their studies and with passage of time achieved what was expected out of them.

Curiously children leaned back on him for help and he provided them. There had been some mistakes but to err is human and he was ready to compensate for them. Time moved at a faster pace. Doctor was firm in sending his children or our children away from parental supervision to exercise their learnings and to compete in the world to gain confidence in their personalities to prosper and also to get a feedback that what they have achieved was on their own, which would boost their strengths to the highest extent. He used to hold meetings within the family to share each other's thoughts, feelings and experiences and would give guidance when asked upon or when he would note that certain deviations are impending. I was happy with the overall progress of the children in all field from scholarly angle to sports, more so with their personality strengths and remained friendly with them. All my children were popular in their circles.

The older girl was very expressive and bold. The middle son was robust, muscular and adventurous and the younger girl was studious and an achiever in academics. Doctor was also friendly but in an authoritative manner. Children would come to me with good news and used to go him with not good news. He was very particular about reporting the adversaries first. Every year we used to go to IPS conferences all sponsored by pharma industries and I failed to forget one incident when in due appreciation of the services provided and as a token of gratitude for entertaining us I handed over one of my gold-plated bracelet to one CEO of some company, which was not pure gold but was mistaken so and the person was reluctant to accept it considering the price of the gift and I was ashamed to get caught by the mere confusion of its originality and worth.

We had differences in opinions about ideologies and were absolute contrasts in particular likes and dislikes. He would watch Hollywood movies and I would watch TV serials of lady's playing leading and dictating roles. I would die for company being a social animal and would attend any number of parties tirelessly and he would prefer solitude and thick volumes of literary books to read alone. I was a talkative chatter box and he was a patient listener. I would want gaudy colors and he would suffice with black and white. I loved exchanging gift and he hated them. I would like to serve guest with exquisite cuisines and he would entertain them by his pseudo-philosophical speeches. I would like to run around and play and he would sit at place and think.

The older girl was given in marriage to US and unfortunately got abused but rescued by Doctor and was remarried in a family with values of heritage. The son was sent to NZ and changed from arrogance to humility and the younger one selected another abusive partner but by grace of God was saved in time, went to US for higher studies, made a good career and got a decent boy from hometown got settled. We had the blessing in the form of grand kids and were contended. Doctor took another wrong decision of course this time under my influence of leaving our home country and migrating at a later time. He knew migration is a stress immaterial of people involved but he took the challenge. He left his busy faculty professional consultancy practice and left the awarded highest cadre of professorship. We all landed from tropical to cold climate and suffered several shocks but absorbed them.

The thing which I missed was lack of gathering, get togethers, parties and shopping sprees along with dependence on hired help, when everything was mandatory to be dome by ourselves. The weather was so unpredictable as though a child throwing tantrums and showing mood swings. The capitalistic governance was a total chaos with admixture of different colored races could live in harmony and were mostly segregated. The rich were becoming filthy rich and the poor were becoming homeless. The kids were rebellious and gun culture prevailed with utmost satisfaction. Violence was loved and somberness disliked. Homo-sexuality was encouraged and same sex marriages became the trend. Churches were empty and gambling dens packed with crowds. Neighbor were unknown and racial discrimination was persistent. Ethics were forgotten and revolts were favored. Cheating was a common business and the system was awful.

Charity was selective and honesty selective. Everyone was in a hurry and kids were left with cartoons to watch. All seem to be living in a virtual world and faraway from reality. Human services were for name sake and health system mediated by middle men. Medical insurance was a havoc and the animal pets were a favorite entity. I had my fears that this culture will be ruined shortly. Vulgarity was appreciated and decency curbed. Menial workers were undocumented but were wanted and hence not deported. The skilled professions were taxed with no privileges given for their expertise. The life here was a mess. I didn't have any responsibility to bring a change and wasn't interested in any renaissance.

I had enough of my personal problems to attend and Doctor was a priority among them. He never or doesn't believe in giving up the means of escape or getting involved in pretentious behaviors, even when it is not necessary to do so and he mostly observing his means to escapism or adventure to buy time. During his trials in continuity to gain time he sometimes becomes intolerable, some times prohibitive and at other times he indulges in fast becoming irrelevant. He would boast as an emperor do with no empire, his vested interests allocating him with divine powers as he believes actually made him into a focus of re-enforced existence of perpetual mania or grandiosity. He was bound to nothing, with no accountability to anyone and underdoing moments becoming his destiny. I also noticed he would penetrate into manipulative environment with his unknown and unfamiliar supporting factors, which are non-existing ultimately becoming a calculated miscalculation. In the end we bad to settle on diametrically opposite dimensions of anhelations and it was a catastrophe in itself.

Printed in the United States
By Bookmasters